RACE AND RACISM

RACE AND RACISM

A Comparative Perspective

Pierre L. van den Berghe

University of Washington

JOHN WILEY & SONS, INC.

NEW YORK · LONDON · SYDNEY

1967

Copyright © 1967 by John Wiley & Sons, Inc.

Library of Congress Catalog Card Number: 67-22553
Printed in the United States of America

To Eric and Oliver with the hope that the world will be saner by the time they grow up.

Acknowledgments

This small book constitutes a distillation of the first and probably the most formative phase of my scholarly career. In a decade of teaching and cross-cultural research in the area of "race relations" I have had enough time to accumulate a staggering intellectual debt. Among the ancestral figures I probably owe most to Weber, Marx, and Durkheim, and, in the more specific area of race, to Park and his "Chicago school." This work is not a rehash of my dissertation; although I am not ashamed of its content, its form is so overladen with the ponderous pedantry that most graduate students think they are expected to produce as to be unreadable for anybody except a tolerant thesis adviser. This role was jointly performed for me by Gordon W. Allport and Talcott Parsons, and, insofar as this book did grow, however indirectly, from my thesis, my debt to them remains quite large. Among the other *gurus* who left a durable impact on my outlook, I should like to mention Georges Balandier, Roger Bastide, and Claude Lévi-Strauss in Paris, Richard T. LaPiere and George Spindler at Stanford, and George Homans, Barrington Moore, Samuel Stouffer, and Clyde Kluckhohn at Harvard. Among the people with whom I associated as colleagues and who became close friends, I owe special gratitude to Leo and Hilda Kuper and to Benjamin and Lore Colby. I am also thankful to my friends and colleagues at the University of Washington, particularly to Ernest A. T. Barth, Frank Miyamoto, and Norman Hayner who read and criticized portions of the manuscript. In addition, friends, informants, research and teaching assistants, secretaries, and students too numerous to mention contributed data, stimulation, and indeed often a feeling of exhilaration in the conduct of my teaching, field work, and writing. Ellin Saito and Linda Reiser had the dubious pleasure of deciphering my scribblings and transforming them into a usable typescript, a task very few could have performed so excellently. Last but not least, my wife Irmgard, aside from her companionship and her sobering editorial comments, provided the logistic support of a smoothly operating household and contained the boisterous vitality of our joint offspring within manageable limits.

Pierre L. van den Berghe

Seattle, Washington
April 1967

Contents

RACE AND RACISM

I

Introduction

The only legitimate excuse for writing a short book about a vast topic on which voluminous literature already exists is the belief that one can contribute, or at least suggest, a fresh approach to the subject. At the same time, such a belief, if not validated by the content of the book, presupposes a great deal of presumptuousness, not to say intellectual narcissism. I have chosen to take the risk of facing that accusation rather than to write a safely eclectic and uncontroversial rehash of the theories and findings of the prevailing "schools" in the area of race relations. This work is thus unashamedly a statement of my personal approach to the subject rather than a textbook-like summary of the field.

A peculiar fascination of the study of "race" is the light it throws on one of the fundamental problems of science, namely, the possibility of an "objective" science free of ideology and values extrinsic to itself. Of course, all but the most naïve of social scientists accept the fact that scientific research has its own ethos or set of values that presumably affects the conduct of inquiry and the norms of scholarly discourse. Many men of science, however, still deny that ideologies and values extrinsic to their discipline and present in the society and epoch of which they are members profoundly affect scientific findings and theories. At

1

the very least many of those who admit that the purity of science may indeed be contaminated by the virus of ideology nevertheless believe that infection is avoidable and that science can be value-free. Belief in the externality of science to the universe it studies, and more particularly of social science to the society from which it evolved, is one of the cornerstones of nineteenth-century positivism.

Having studied race relations for a decade, I have been driven to abandon the comfort of positivism and to regard scientific objectivity as a chimera. To pretend that we can operate in a value vacuum when assuming the role of the scientist is, I believe, a naïve delusion which may lead us to *hide* our biases but not to eliminate their effect on our thinking. I therefore beg my readers to take this book *cum grano salis,* as I shall try to do with the work of my distinguished colleagues.

This seeming digression was necessary because of the special nature of race relations as a field of study. Contamination of science by ideology is not equally serious and obvious in each of its various areas. Presumably, it affects astronomy to a lesser extent than sociology; and in the field of sociology the area of race has been among the most thoroughly permeated by extrinsic values. From the middle of the nineteenth century until the 1920s when the Western *Weltanschauung* was infected by racism and social Darwinism, the study of race and race relations generally exhibited the same characteristics. (A few towering figures, like the anthropologist Franz Boas, stand out as exceptions.) In the 1930s, when cultural relativism, anti-racism, and the attribution of overwhelming determinism to the social environment became fashionable, specialists in race relations became the vanguard of liberal intellectuals eager to expose the folly and the crimes of the past. Let me hasten to add that I am myself a product of this climate of anti-racism and social environmentalism, but hopefully I am a conscious product of it.

Critique of Dominant Trends in the Study of Race Relations

Before sketching an alternative approach to race relations, I shall characterize the dominant trends in this area of social science. I shall avoid mentioning names because to lump individualistic scholars in a "school" necessarily arouses vehement protests. I do argue, however, that the majority of North American or North American-influenced scholars (who between them are responsible for the bulk of the scientific output in this area) exhibit most of the following characteristics. Naturally, a few have remained clearly distinct from the mainstream.

1. In reaction against the patently pseudo-scientific notions of nineteenth-century European and American racists and social Darwinists a new orthodoxy developed. Its major tenets were (a) that phenotypical or genotypical differences between subspecies of *homo sapiens* (insofar as such subspecies could be determined at all) were not significantly related to any differences in intelligence or any other socially meaningful capability and (b) that individual and, to an even greater degree, group differences between people were predominantly (though not exclusively) the result of the social environment (i.e., the family milieu, the culture, and the society at large) as opposed to heredity or the physical environment such as climate and topography.

Scholars dissenting with these two postulates have been voices in the wilderness (except, of course, in Nazi Germany, South Africa, and the American South) and their views have been dismissed as perverse or preposterous. Not unexpectedly, the overwhelming weight of evidence supports the two postulates of the new orthodoxy. Although I certainly share these beliefs, I am not overly impressed with the evidence; indeed, to contemporaries of Gobineau and Chamberlain, it seemed to point the other way. To be sure, today's evidence has improved over that of the nineteenth century but not enough to provide for total comfort and complacency.

The negative case is instructive here, namely, what happened when the *prima facie* evidence contradicted the scientific credo; for example, when I.Q. tests showed wide differences between racial groups. The highest critical standards were applied and the most stringent controls for social variables were introduced to demonstrate, often successfully, that much if not all of the difference was a function of disparities in the social environment [1]. Although this line of inquiry is convincing enough, we would

certainly wish that the *prima facie* evidence in favor of the orthodoxy would be subjected to the same degree of scrutiny and rigor.
Instead, "favorable" evidence has often been readily accepted,
even when extremely tenuous and "soft," provided it met the
test of plausibility and intuitive meaning. Thus the widely held
belief that racial discrimination and prejudice are damaging to
the personality of Negroes is based on some questionable psychoanalytical data from a few chosen clinical cases [2], and on much
subjective experience and common sense. Yet the data were considered sound enough for the proposition to influence social
action and to be cited as evidence in the appendix to the 1954
Supreme Court decision against school segregation.

In point of fact, both postulates are extremely difficult to prove
in any strict manner with the techniques at our disposal and our
self-imposed limitations on experimentation with human beings.
The first tenet, namely the absence of significant group differences in capabilities, is intrinsically unprovable by standard statistical methods that are based on a "null-hypothesis" rationale.
As any statistician knows, failure to reject the null hypothesis
does not allow us to accept it [3]. Proof of the second tenet is
made extremely difficult by the near impossibility of holding
either social or nonsocial factors constant. Identical twin studies
do control the genetic factor to the best of our knowledge but not
the nonhuman environment.

2. Much of the literature on race relations during the last
three decades has dealt with the United States and has been
written by scholars who lacked comparative experience. (Notable
exceptions include the works of Oliver C. Cox, Franklin Frazier,
Melville Herskovits, Frank Tannenbaum, Gilberto Freyre, Gonzalo Aguirre Beltrán, Charles Wagley, Marvin Harris, Andrew
W. Lind, Tamotsu Shibutani, Kian Kwan, and Leo and Hilda
Kuper [4]). For every hundred published racial attitude studies
done in the United States, we could perhaps find five to ten in
all the rest of the world. This lack of comparative approach has
led, among other things, to an implicit or explicit overgenerali-
zation of American findings. In addition, culture-bound instru-
ments (such as the "F" scale) have been applied uncritically to
other cultures; consequently, lack of sophistication in comparative methodology has adversely affected the quality of much of

the little cross-cultural research that has been conducted. Indeed, the field of comparative race relations is so incoherent and embryonic that almost any cross-cultural study, however poorly designed and executed, is destined to be regarded as "pioneering." The scarcity of sociological literature (as distinct from descriptive ethnography and history) on such important multi-racial or multi-ethnic societies as, for example, Peru, Mexico, and Indonesia, is disheartening.

3. Many race scholars have limited themselves not only in space but also in time. Sociologists have concentrated on contemporary industrial societies without much concern for, or knowledge of, the past. Anthropologists have often displayed antiquarian zeal for reconstructing indigenous societies in their pristine preconquest purity, but, except for the Mexican school of anthropology, they have generally failed to relate these ethnic minorities meaningfully to the total society that engulfed them [5]. Historians have, of course, been concerned with the past, but the bulk of American historiography has until the last twenty or twenty-five years displayed ethnocentrism, if not racism, and has ignored, understressed, or badly distorted many issues, institutions, or processes related to race. Only recently, under the influence of such writers as C. Vann Woodward, Oscar Handlin, John Hope Franklin, Richard Hofstadter, and Frank Tannenbaum, has a more balanced picture of American history emerged [6]. Moreover, many American historians have defined the substantive scope of their discipline in narrowly political, economic, and military terms, leaving us in the dark about the social life of the past, including, of course, race relations.

Many sociologists who have studied American race relations (with the exception of people like Robert E. Park and Gunnar Myrdal) [7] have lacked a historical perspective, not in the sense that they were unaware of basic historical facts but rather that they did not comprehend the evolutionary dynamics of American race relations and the revolutionary import of the Reconstruction Era. It took a Latin American like Gilberto Freyre to show that the similarities between slavery regimes in Brazil, the southern United States, and the West Indies overshadowed discontinuities over time *within* these countries [8].

4. The field of race relations has been generally characterized

by a high degree of emphasis on practical policy applications, a low degree of theoretical integration with the rest of sociology, and a high degree of analytical isolation of race from its general social context. The concern for practical applications of research is, of course, perfectly legitimate; however, it has often resulted in a definition of research problems and an allocation of scientific resources in terms of immediate policy goals rather than in terms of contribution to whatever corpus of theory exists in the social sciences. Few scholars in the area have risen above what Robert Merton has called "theories of the middle range" and many have contentedly remained at the level of empirical generalizations, description, or narrowly defined studies of problems such as demographic correlates of race relations and the methodology of racial attitude scales. Despite a great amount of valuable research the field of race relations has come to resemble a theoretical no-man's-land between psychology, sociology, and anthropology [9].

Part of the reluctance of "race" scholars to indulge in theory construction may be the fear of cogitating themselves out of a specialty. Or, phrased differently, the failure to arrive at a theory of race relations may simply reflect the fact that the subject has no theoretical leg to stand on. Indeed, we could make a strong case for the position that race is only an interesting special case in a broad range of similar phenomena, hence has little claim for autonomous theoretical status. Thus a sociologist might regard racial distinctions as a special case of invidious status differentiation, and a social psychologist might consider racial attitudes as a specific expression of the much wider syndrome of prejudice. It would not seem fruitful to try to subsume under a single theoretical umbrella a phenomenon such as race which can so readily be broken down into analytical components, each of which in turn can be articulated in existing bodies of more general theory.

If one accepts, as I do, that race is only a special case of more general social facts, it follows that there can be no general theory of race and that race relations must be placed within the total institutional and cultural context of the society studied. A few sociologists like R. E. Park, Gunnar Myrdal, Robin Williams, and Oliver C. Cox have from a variety of perspectives related race relations to such basic elements of social or cultural structure as stratification, ideology, the distribution of power, and the system of production; most, however, have adopted a piecemeal rather than a holistic approach.

5. Finally, in spite of the claim of many social scientists that detachment and objectivity are possible and that they can dissociate their roles as scientists and as private citizens, much of the work done by North Americans in the area of race has, until the last three or four years, been strongly flavored with a great deal of optimism and complacency about the basic "goodness" of American society and with the cautious, slightly left-of-center, reformist, meliorative, gradualist approach of "liberal" intellectuals. In a recent article John Horton spells out the characteristics of "order" and "conflict" theories in the field of race relations and argues that American social scientists have leaned heavily toward political liberalism, which is a variant of conservative order theory [10]. The field has been dominated by a functionalist view of society and a definition of the race problem as one of integration and assimilation of minorities into the mainstream of a consensus-based society.

Thus much of the applied work in the field has been directed at changing prejudicial attitudes rather than discriminatory behavior, despite the fact that this strategy has proven slow, expensive, and limited in its effectiveness; on the other hand, the elimination of discrimination has typically been followed by rapid changes in attitudes. At a more theoretical level race relations in the United States have, following Myrdal's lead [11], been interpreted more often as a moral dilemma in the hearts and minds of men rather than a complex dynamic of group conflict resulting from the differential distribution of power, wealth, prestige, and other social rewards [12].

At the verbal level there have been some statements of awareness of the problem of objectivity. Since the publication of *An American Dilemma* [13] it has become fashionable to state one's value position explicitly, but the reader is sometimes left with the impression that this is a kind of exorcism, or intellectual purification ritual, by which the author purges his thinking of ideological contamination rather than an admission that values and science are inextricably intertwined.

In the last three or four years, with the rather sudden swing of vocal segments of the American Negro leadership away from integration and consensus and toward a more militant ideology of group identity and conflict, there has been a remarkable shift in the intellectual climate of social scientists specializing in this field. Optimism becomes stigmatized as naïve, conventional liberal ideology is increasingly questioned, and conflict theory is becoming fashionable, even though conflict is still generally regarded as undesirable and the accent is still put on conflict resolution. In the race relations field, more than in many others, social science theory is little more than a weathercock shifting with ideological winds.

The sources of the limitations I have just outlined are numerous, but least among them is the incompetence of the scholars involved. Given the relative development of the social sciences in the United States and the salience of race in that society, it is not surprising that North Americans have dominated this specialty. Inadequate knowledge of foreign languages, relative lack of American involvement in an overseas colonial empire, and other factors of cultural and intellectual isolation go a long way to account for the lack of comparative perspective of most American scholars. The intellectual credo of positivism or realism, the reaction against nineteenth-century social evolutionism, and the epistemological antithesis between "science" and "history" contributed to some of the other limitations.

Beyond these underlying background factors, individual motivations further complicated the picture. Most specialists in race relations have been very *engagé,* either as angry members of subjugated groups or as guilt-ridden members of a privileged group trying to atone for the sins of their forebears. *Engagé* as they were, they mostly adhered to an ideology of positivism which made them simulate detachment and objectivity, often to the point of convincing themselves that they had been successful in their search for intellectual Nirvana. The most self-deceptive fiction toward that end is the notion that one can dissociate one's role as scientist from that of private citizen or separate objective appraisals from policy recommendations. Theoretically we can, of course, but practically we often cannot, and what good does it do to pretend that we have?

Some Definitions

These remarks, critical as they are, should not be interpreted as a blanket indictment or as a denial that a great deal of valuable work has been done in the area. Rather, they should be accepted as a self-imposed challenge to remedy some of these shortcomings or at least to suggest a more holistic, historical, systematic and comparative approach. Before discussing this approach, however, a few basic terms have to be defined.

The term "race" has been quite confusing because of its four principal connotations.

1. Physical anthropologists have called races the various subspecies of *homo sapiens* characterized by certain phenotypical and genotypical traits (e.g., the "Mongoloid race" or the "Negroid race"). They have not agreed among themselves, and biological classifications of the human species include three to more than a score of such races [14]. Belatedly, many physical anthropologists are abandoning racial taxonomies altogether.

2. Laymen have profusely used the word race to describe a human group that shared certain cultural characteristics such as language or religion (e.g., the "French race" or the "Jewish race").

3. Race has been loosely used as a synonym for species (e.g., the "human race").

4. Many social scientists have meant by race a human group that defines itself and/or is defined by other groups as different from other groups by virtue of innate and immutable physical characteristics. These physical characteristics are in turn believed to be intrinsically related to moral, intellectual, and other nonphysical attributes or abilities.

Here, we consistently use the term race in its fourth meaning to refer to a group that is *socially* defined but on the basis of *physical* criteria. The first meaning has little if any relevance to the last and does not concern us here. Neither does the third meaning. To distinguish the second usage from the fourth, we designate the second "ethnic groups" or "ethnicities." Ethnic groups, like races in the fourth connotation, are socially defined but on the basis of *cultural* criteria. In practice, the distinction between a racial and an ethnic group is sometimes blurred by several facts. Cultural traits are often regarded as genetic and inherited (e.g., body odor, which is a function of diet, cosmetics, and other cultural items); physical appearance can be culturally changed (by scarification, surgery, and cosmetics); and the sensory perception of physical differences is affected by cultural definitions of race (e.g., a rich Negro may be seen as lighter than an equally dark poor Negro, as suggested by the Brazilian proverb: "Money bleaches"). However, the distinction between race and ethnicity remains analytically useful.

The confusion arising from the various usages of race has led some authors, like W. Lloyd Warner, to avoid the word altogether and to describe race relations in *caste* terms [15]. Adopting Kroeber's "minimum" definition of caste as an endogamous and hierarchized group in which one is born and out of which one cannot move, Warner speaks of whites and Negroes in the United States as castes separated by a "caste line." Each of two castes is internally subdivided into permeable classes (upper, middle, and lower).

This approach, shared by Allison Davis, B. B. Gardner, and M. R. Gardner, Gunnar Myrdal, and others, has been criticized by O. C. Cox, who took the position that the Hindu caste system was unique and that the term caste should not be applied loosely to other quite different situations [16]. A fundamental difference between the Hindu system and that of the United States, according to Cox, is that the Hindu system of inequality is (or at least was until recently) based on consent, whereas that of the United States was characterized by conflict. Cox is undoubtedly right in stressing the importance of the consent-conflict dimension, but he is incorrect in opposing the Indian and the American situations as he does. Indian history saw a succession of reform movements against caste and of intercaste struggles for supremacy or prestige. Conversely, in the ante-bellum South slavery was accompanied by a considerable degree of accommodation of Negroes to their inferior status and by a lower degree of overt and violent conflict than in the post-bellum period.

In my estimation the controversy boils down to a question of definitions. I do not regard the word race as objectionable, provided its reference to a *social* group is clear. At the same time, race relations in the United States, South Africa, and other areas have exhibited significant caste-like properties, so that the use of the word caste in this context also seems appropriate. Caste in its minimum sense then becomes an analytical and comparative concept applicable to a number of societies rather than a unique historical label. When it is necessary to differentiate Hindu caste from minimum caste, I shall speak of "racial castes" or "color castes."

The last key term to define is "racism." In modern American usage the word is often used to refer to the virulent brand of the disease, that is, to intense, overt, violent hatred of racial "out-groups." Here, we adopt a wider definition. Racism is any set of beliefs that organic, genetically transmitted differences (whether real or imagined) between human groups are intrinsically associated with the presence or the absence of certain socially relevant abilities or characteristics, hence that such differences are a legitimate basis of invidious distinctions between groups socially defined as races [17]. According to these definitions of race and racism, it is clear that the two concepts are closely related. The existence of races in a given society presupposes the presence of racism, for without racism physical characteristics are devoid of social significance. It is not the presence of objective physical differences between groups that creates races, but the social recognition of such differences as socially significant or relevant. We return to this point in a later section of this chapter.

Origins and Distribution of Racism

Until a few years ago it was not intellectually respectable among many American social scientists to ask the question: How did a social phenomenon get started? This ahistorical and anti-evolutionary attitude was a reaction against the simplistic, uni-linear evolutionism of the late nineteenth century. Such questions were intrinsically unanswerable, I was told as a graduate student, either because they were of the "chicken and the egg" variety or because the origins of social institutions were lost in the night of time, hence any attempt at historical reconstruction was un-scientific and speculative.

First, it is important to stress that racism, unlike ethnocentrism, is not a universal phenomenon. Members of all human societies have a fairly good opinion of themselves compared with members of other societies, but this good opinion is frequently based on claims to cultural superiority. Man's claims to excellence are usually narcissistically based on his own creations. Only a few human groups have deemed themselves superior because of the content of their gonads. Of course, racist cultures have also been ethnocentric, and some peoples have held the theory that their cultures were superior because of their superior genetic pool. But the reverse is not true: many, indeed most, societies have exhibited ethnocentrism without racism.

On the other hand, the contention that racism is a unique in-vention of nineteenth-century Western European culture and its colonial offshoots in the Americas, Australia, Africa, and Asia is also untrue. Racism, as might be expected of such a crude idea, has been independently discovered and rediscovered by various peoples at various times in history. For example, in the traditional kingdoms of Rwanda and Burundi in the Great Lakes area of central Africa the Tutsi aristocracy (about 15 per cent of the population) ruled over the Hutu majority and a small group of Twa. The three groups are physically distinguishable: the Twa are a Pygmoid group of shorter stature and somewhat lighter complexion than the Negroid Hutu; the Tutsi, although as dark as the Hutu, are by far the tallest group and have distinctly non-Negroid features. Of course, miscegenation over three centuries of Tutsi domination has somewhat blurred these physical dis-tinctions, but, nevertheless, physical characteristics, notably height, play a prominent role in the Tutsi claim to superiority and political domination.

The Muslim emirates of Northern Nigeria, where a Fulani aristocracy conquered the local Hausa in the first decade of the nineteenth century, provide another illustration of non-Western racism, albeit only a mild manifestation. Thus M. G. Smith writes about one of the vassal states of Sokoto in northern Nigeria: "In Zaria also, social significance is given to color distinctions; value is placed on lightness of skin as an attribute of beauty, and as a racial character, and a host of qualitative terms reflect this interest, such as *ja-jawur* (light-copper skin), *baki* (dark), *baki kirim,* or *baki swal* (real black), and so forth. The Fulani rulers of Zaria distinguish on racial grounds between themselves and their Hausa subjects, stressing such features as skin color, hair, and facial form, and also make similar distinctions among themselves, since past miscegenation has produced wide physical differences among them" [18].

Allowing, then, for the independent discovery of racism in a number of societies, it remains true that the Western strain of the virus has eclipsed all others in importance. Through the colonial expansion of Europe racism spread widely over the world. Apart from its geographical spread, no other brand of racism has developed such a flourishing mythology and ideology. In folklore, as well as in literature and science, racism became a deeply ingrained component of the Western *Weltanschauung.* Western racism had its poets like Kipling, its philosophers like Gobineau and Chamberlain, its statesmen like Hitler, Theodore Roosevelt, and Verwoerd; this is a record not even remotely approached in either scope or complexity by any other cultural tradition. Therefore, in this book, we shall concentrate on Western racism.

Let us ask again the question of the origin of racism in the specific context of the Western tradition. Two major ways of answering the question are in terms of necessary antecedent conditions and efficient causes. The most important necessary (but not sufficient) condition for the rise of racism is the presence in sufficient numbers of two or more groups that look different enough so that at least some of their members can be readily classifiable. In addition to their physical differences, these groups also have to be culturally different (at least when they first met) and in a position of institutionalized inequality for the idea of inherent racial differences to take root. It seems that only when group differences in race overlap at least partly with dissimilarities in status and culture are these two sets of differences held to be causally related to one another.

These conditions are most clearly met when groups come into contact through migration, of which the most common types are the following:

1. Military conquest in which the victor (often in numerical minority) establishes his political and economic domination over an indigenous group (e.g., the European powers in tropical Africa, starting in the 1870s).

2. Gradual frontier expansion of one group which pushes back and exterminates the native population (e.g., European expansion in North America or Australia), as contrasted with the "dominating symbiosis" of type 1.

3. Involuntary migration in which a slave or indentured alien group is introduced into a country to constitute a servile caste (e.g., the slave regimes of the United States, Brazil, and the West Indies).

4. Voluntary migration when alien groups move into the host country to seek political protection or economic opportunities (e.g., Puerto Rican, Mexican, or Cuban immigration to the United States mainland or West Indian immigration into Britain).

These various forms of migration, singly or in combination, account for most of the interracial societies created by Western powers and indeed probably also for most non-Western societies in which racism is present. However, the migration (whether peaceful or military, voluntary or involuntary) of culturally and physically different groups does not tell the whole story. Indeed, there have been many cases in which these conditions were met but in which racism did not develop. This is true despite the fact that such pluralistic societies are often rigidly stratified and characterized by acute ethnic competition and conflict. Thus, for example, the Spanish conquest of the New World, brutal as it was, gave rise to only a mild form of racism toward Indians, although religious bigotry and ethnocentricism were dominant traits of the Spanish outlook. Similarly, the Aryan invasion of India, although it probably marked the beginnings of the Hindu caste system, does not appear to have brought about racism. Some scholars argue that mild racism exists in India and underlies the origin of the caste system. *Varna* (the broad division into four groups of castes: Brahmin, Kshatriya, Vaisya, and Sudra) literally means "color"; Hinduism uses the same kind of color symbolism as the Judeo-Christian tradition, associating evil with black and good with white; and there is a mild esthetic preference for lighter skin in modern Indian culture. But this is very much of a limiting case.

Given the necessary and facilitating conditions for the development of racism, what are the efficient causes of it? It seems probable that in each historical case in which racism appeared its causal antecedents have been different. Here, I shall try to answer the question only with reference to Western racism, a difficult enough problem in itself. A number of fragmentary answers have been advanced by various social scientists, most of them ascribing causal priority according to their theoretical predilection. Thus to a psychologist the ultimate source or "seat" of racism is personality, and causation must be sought in terms of the dynamics of frustration and aggression, or the "authoritarian personality." We shall return to the psychological aspects of racism, but our primary concern at present is with the *social* level of explanation.

Vulgar Marxism has a monocausal theory on the origin of racism; racism is part of the bourgeois ideology designed especially to rationalize the exploitation of nonwhite peoples of the world during the imperialistic phase of capitalism. Racist ideology thus becomes simply an epiphenomenon symptomatic of slavery and colonial exploitation. In the modern American context vulgar Marxists have interpreted racism as a capitalist device to divide the working class into two hostile segments for better control. Others, more inclined to assign causal priority to the realm of ideas, trace the origins of racism to the current of social Darwinism and the reaction against eighteenth-century environmentalism.

Western racism is a fairly well-defined historical phenomenon, characteristic of a distinct epoch; it came of age in the third or fourth decade of the nineteenth century, achieved its golden age approximately between 1880 and 1920, and has since entered its period of decline, although, of course, its lingering remains are likely to be with us at least for the next three or four decades. To be sure, racist ideas were occasionally expressed in the eighteenth century and even before. Thus Thomas Jefferson wrote in his *Notes on Virginia* (1782): "This unfortunate difference of color, and perhaps of faculty, is a powerful obstacle to the emancipation of these people [i.e., Negroes]." In various places Jefferson described Negroes in the following terms: "In music they are more generally gifted than the whites." "They seem to require less sleep." "They secrete less by the kidneys, and more by the glands of the skin, which gives them a very strong and disagreeable odor." Even the Spanish of the sixteenth and seventeenth centuries, who have a reputation for lack of racism, did exhibit it in mild form, but it was almost invariably intertwined with, and secondary to, ethnocentrism.

The era of the Enlightenment which immediately preceded the growth of racism was strongly environmentalist (i.e., the belief was that both the physical and social environment determined human behavior to a greater extent than heredity), and Jefferson himself never resolved this intellectual dilemma to his satisfaction. He continuously wavered between racist and social "explanations" of group differences. Racist thinking in the Anglo-Saxon world, in Germany, and to a lesser extent in other European countries was in the ascendancy in the 1830s and 1840s; throughout the second half of the century it retained the status of a firmly established, respectable orthodoxy, and it received the accolade of science, both natural and social, in the United States, Canada, Britain, Australia, Germany, and to some degree in the Low Countries and France. Two great classics of racist literature are Arthur de Gobineau's *Essai sur l'Inégalité des Races Humaines,* published in 1853–1855, and in 1911, Houston Stuart Chamberlain's *The Foundations of Nineteenth Century.* Lesser luminaries like Adolf Hitler and Theodore Roosevelt also penned substantial contributions to the field, but, unlike their armchair predecessors, applied their ideas with a considerable degree of success.

Any social explanation of the genesis of Western racism must, I believe, take three main factors into account.

1. Racism was congruent with prevailing forms of capitalist exploitation, notably with slavery in the New World and incipient colonial expansion in Africa. There is no question that the desire to rationalize exploitation of non-European peoples

fostered the elaboration of a complex ideology of paternalism and racism, with its familiar themes of grownup childishness, civilizing mission, atavistic savagery, and arrested evolution. However, any simple, direct, causal relationship that makes racism an epiphenomenal derivative of the system of production is unsatisfactory. European chattel slavery antedated the development of racist thinking; it was not until the nineteenth century that racism became a well-defined ideology distinguishable from ethnocentrism. Of course, the dehumanizing effect of slavery on both slave and owner facilitated the view of the Negro as a beast of burden without culture, and racism was a convenient rationalization for both slavery and colonialism. Yet both slavery and colonialism existed, as far as we know, without an appreciable amount of racism; therefore racism cannot be accounted for purely as a consequence of slavery and colonialism.

2. Racism was congruent with the new Darwinian current of thought in the biological sciences [19]. Notions of stages of evolution, survival of the fittest, hereditary determinism, and near constancy of the gene pool (except for rare mutations) were all eagerly applied to *homo sapiens* and adopted by the bourgeois social science of the late nineteenth century, represented by such figures as Herbert Spencer and William Graham Sumner. Social Darwinism and organicism (i.e., the notion that society is analogous to biological organisms) also dovetailed with the economic liberalism of the early nineteenth century. Although John Stuart Mill and other early liberals were explicitly antiracists, *laissez-faire* was later reinterpreted as a mandate not to interfere with any form of human inequality and suffering. The poor were poor because they were biologically inferior; Negroes were slaves as a result of natural selection which had found the best place for them. Thus philanthropy, abolitionism, or any other attempt to interfere with "nature" could only debilitate the superior race by favoring inferior people (who already had the nasty habit of reproducing like rabbits, perhaps to compensate for their deservedly high mortality rate).

3. The egalitarian and libertarian ideas of the Enlightenment spread by the American and French Revolutions conflicted, of course, with racism, but they also paradoxically contributed to its development. Faced with the blatant contradiction between

the treatment of slaves and colonial peoples and the official
rhetoric of freedom and equality, Europeans and white North
Americans began to dichotomize humanity between men and
submen (or the "civilized" and the "savages"). The scope of applicability of the egalitarian ideals was restricted to "the people,"
that is, the whites, and there resulted what I have called *"Herrenvolk* democracies,"—regimes such as those of the United States or
South Africa that are democratic for the master race but tyranni-
cal for the subordinate groups [20]. The desire to preserve both
the profitable forms of discrimination and exploitation and the
democratic ideology made it necessary to deny humanity to the
oppressed groups. It is only an apparent paradox that the lot of
the slave has typically been better in aristocratic societies (like
colonial Latin America or many traditional African kingdoms
that practiced domestic slavery) than in *Herrenvolk* democracies
like the United States.

Race and Personality

Because racism is ultimately reducible to a set of attitudes
which are, of course, socially derived but which nevertheless
become part of the personality system of the individual, the study
of race relations is as fully within the scope of social psychology
as it is within that of sociology [21]. The emphasis of this book
on historical and sociological factors certainly does not mean that
the psychological approach to the problem is unimportant, or
even secondary, to the sociological or historical approach. The
virtual exclusion of psychology here is simply a matter of arbitrary definition of the scope of the book, and this in turn is partly
a consequence of my own disciplinary limitations. However, a
summary statement of the relationship between the psychology
and the sociology of race relations is indispensable.

Psychologists have done an impressive amount of research in
the United States (and to a lesser extent elsewhere) on the psychology of prejudice and of group differences. This work has
ranged from quantitative studies of group differences in intelligence and other individual characteristics to qualitative and
interpretative psychoanalytical accounts of the underlying psy-

chodynamics of prejudice [22]. I shall be concerned here primarily with two fundamental questions in this area.

1. Why do certain persons become racially prejudiced and others do not?
2. How is the internalization of prejudice at the personality level related to the social morphology of racism?

Two main and somewhat related answers have been given to the first question: the "frustration-aggression" and the "authoritarian personality" theories. In simplest terms the frustration-aggression argument is as follows: denial of certain goals or gratifications leads to frustration, which is, at least in some situations, displaced from the causal agent of the frustration to an unrelated scapegoat. The scapegoat then becomes the object of aggressive behavior, and this expression of aggression presumably has the cathartic effect of relieving frustration. When the choice of scapegoats becomes culturally stabilized on members of certain groups, racial or ethnic prejudice results because the expression of aggression is rationalized in terms of the alleged undesirable traits of the scapegoats [23].

Like the frustration-aggression theory, the authoritarian personality approach is strongly anchored in psychoanalytical concepts. According to the authors of *The Authoritarian Personality,* a syndrome exists which predisposes certain persons to become prejudiced against members of ethnic and racial groups. Among the traits characteristic of the authoritarian personality are respect for force, submission toward superiors, aggression toward subordinates, lack of self-insight, acceptance of ready-made ideas, intolerance of deviance, destructiveness and cynicism, a tendency toward superstition, and an "exaggerated" interest in sex. Presumably these traits develop in early childhood, largely as a consequence of the family environment. Persons exhibiting these traits, as detected by the "F" scale, also tend to score highly on scales (such as the "E" scale) designed to measure the degree of hostility toward out-groups such as Jews and Negroes [24].

Both psychological approaches to racial prejudice have been the object of an abundant critical literature, a review of which would take more space than is necessary for our purposes. Suffice it to say that there is considerable experimental, clinical, and questionnaire evidence for both approaches, but both have distinct limitations. When social variables are held constant, many correlations become lower; even at the psychological level, neither approach can make any claim to being *the* explanation of prejudice.

To arrive at a better understanding of the psychogenesis and psychodynamics of prejudice, we must relate these problems to the social context, that is, answer the second of the questions raised earlier. Accepting that highly frustrated persons and authoritarians are more likely to be bigots, these factors, by themselves, will often prove to be poor predictors of racial attitudes and discrimination. Clearly, in societies such as South Africa or the southern United States, in which racial bigotry and discrimination by whites are constantly rewarded (in terms of approval, prestige, wealth, and power) and tolerance, liberalism, and "color-blindness" are severely punished, most members of the dominant group will exhibit both prejudice and discrimination, almost irrespective of personality factors. To be sure, even in such societies, the most virulent bigots (e.g., members of lynch mobs) are probably recruited from authoritarians, and, conversely, a number of tolerant persons may discriminate out of habit and social conformity without being prejudiced [25]. However, taking the dominant group as a whole, personality factors will prove a poor predictor of either prejudice or discrimination because racism is a rewarding ideology and a profitable way of life.

However, in societies in which there is latent racism, but whose official norms favor nondiscrimination and blatant expressions of prejudice meet with at least mild disapproval, personality factors are likely to become much better predictors of prejudice and discrimination. In other words, when social pressures and rewards for racism are absent, racial bigotry is more likely to be restricted to people for whom prejudice fulfills a psychological "need." In such a tolerant milieu prejudiced persons may even refrain from discriminating to escape social disapproval. To borrow Robert Merton's terminology, the "prejudiced nondiscriminator" is the mirror image in a tolerant society of the "unprejudiced discriminator" in a racist society. Both types are behavioral conformists, irrespective of their attitudes.

Many studies have demonstrated the importance of social (as distinguished from psychological) determinism in the genesis and maintenance of prejudice. Pettigrew, for example, showed that the much higher degree of anti-Negro prejudice among Southern whites as compared with Northern whites could not be accounted for in terms of differences in authoritarianism between the two groups [26]. Other studies have shown how most "tolerant" persons rapidly assimilate prejudicial norms when they move to a social environment supportive of bigotry and, vice versa, how prejudiced people become tolerant in a nonracist milieu [27].

In summary, there is unquestionably a psychopathology of racism, but in racist societies most racists are not "sick." They simply conform to social norms without "internalizing" their prejudices at any depth. Racism for some people is a symptom of deeply rooted psychological problems, but for most people living in racist societies racial prejudice is merely a special kind of convenient rationalizations for rewarding behavior. If this were not true, racial attitudes would not be so rapidly changeable as they are under changing social conditions [28]. The "sociopathology" of racism is thus a different problem altogether from its psychopathology and one of wider proportions. This analytical distinction may be obscured in reality because the two main dimensions of racism are nearly always intertwined. Obviously, for psychopathology to express itself at the symptomatic level in racial prejudice there has to be *some* racism present in the given society. *Beyond this minimum threshold,* I would hypothesize that *the more overt, blatant, and socially sanctioned racism is, the less of the variance in both racial prejudice and discrimination can be accounted for in psychodynamic terms.* As a simple illustration, to be a member of the White Citizens' Council in Montgomery, Alabama, is no more indicative of psychopathology than being a Rotarian or a Lion in Portland, Oregon, but the reverse would not be true.

Race as a Special Case of Differentiation and Stratification

Race, of course, has no intrinsic significance, except to a racist. To a social scientist, race acquires meaning only through its social definition in a given society. As suggested earlier, race with its social attributes can most fruitfully be regarded as a special case that shares many characteristics with related instances within a broader category of social phenomena. This means that the study of race has little claim for an autonomous theoretical status. A salient aspect of multiracial societies is that racial groups are almost invariably hierarchized in terms of prestige, wealth, and power. Hence race can be treated as a special case of invidious status differentiation or a special criterion of stratification.

Frequently, ethnic groups within a society are also stratified in much the same way as racial groups, as shown, for example, in the colonial societies of Spanish America and, indeed, even today in the less hispanicized parts of such countries as Guatemala, Peru, Bolivia, Ecuador, and Mexico. The resemblance between ethnic and racial pluralism may be so close that it raises the question whether one is dealing with race or ethnicity. In the virtual absence of cultural differences (e.g., between Negro and white North Americans) the answer is unambiguous enough, but the definition of group membership often includes both cultural and physical criteria (e.g., in Brazil).

When cultural criteria of group differentiation are exclusively or predominantly resorted to, there results a more flexible system of stratification than one based on race, for culture can be learned and movement from one ethnic group to another is thus possible. Racial stratification, on the other hand, results in a nearly impermeable caste system more easily than ethnic stratification; race thus represents an extreme case of ascribed status and lack of social mobility. There are even instances of ethnic segmentation without any clear-cut hierarchy of groups, whereas it would be difficult to find an analogous situation in which the criterion is racial. Thus, in spite of considerable anti-Semitic, anti-Catholic, and anti-gentile prejudice, the religious groups in the United States represent simple segmentation rather than hierarchy.

As a special instance of stratification, race shares many characteristics with ethnicity and class. The psychodynamics of prejudice, the mechanisms of social control used by the dominant group, the etiquette of intergroup behavior, the stereotypy and rationalization of discrimination, the patterns of avoidance and of social or spatial distance, all seem to vary independently from the basis of group definition.

To confuse matters further, phenotypical imagery has often been attached to basically ethnic or class distinctions, if only for identification purposes. Thus one is said to look "Jewish" or "Italian," that is, physically distinguishable from other ethnic groups. In nineteenth-century European literature, for example, frequent references are made to distinguishing physical traits between social classes: aquiline noses, slender hands, tapering fingers, small feet, tall, erect, and slender stature, and long and narrow faces with delicate features were regarded as aristocratic; coarseness of traits, squat stature, and large and broad hands and feet were supposed to characterize the peasantry. Sometimes, of course, physical traits such as calluses, developed muscles, body odors, or suntanned faces are determined by occupation or diet and can be accurate indicators of class or ethnicity. (People in the Paris Métro *do* smell different from people in a Calcutta bazaar if only because garlic smells different from curry.)

Real or fancied physical differences between groups, even when a high degree of awareness exists, do not automatically lead to a system of racial castes. Frequently, such differences are only casually referred to or used as convenient identifying characteristics. *Only when group differences in physical traits are considered a determinant of social behavior and moral or intellectual qualities can we properly speak of racism;* only insofar as these differences are seized on as rationalizations for prejudice and discrimination do we find racial castes. Of course, when recognized differences in physical appearance tend to coincide with ethnic groups or social classes, a system of racial castes can easily develop, as, for example, in the first two or three decades of Dutch settlement at the Cape of Good Hope.

Nevertheless, the sheer unequal coexistence of two or more groups that look objectively different does not constitute a system of race relations. Even though phenotypical characteristics may coincide closely with class or ethnic ones, the social definition of the group can be cultural and not racial. Thus tens of thousands of people live in Paris who in the United States would be regarded as "Negroes." For the most part they are not assimilated in the dominant French society and do not enjoy full equal status with the indigenous population. Yet they are not socially defined as a race by most native Frenchmen; depending on their cultural background, they are referred to as Africans,

Malagasi, North Americans, Brazilians, or West Indians. Although these people encounter subtle forms of discrimination and some natives are racists, it would be incorrect to refer to the interaction between blacks and whites in Paris as a system of race relations. Existing discrimination reflects the very high level of ethnocentrism and xenophobia in French society. A Belgian or a Swiss is the object of as much cultural condescension and even ridicule as a Senegalese or Congolese, and the Negro American who may misinterpret discrimination in racial terms is in fact discriminated against *qua* American, not *qua* Negro.

Conversely, racial castes sometimes exist even though physical differences are not sufficient to distinguish reliably between members of various groups. *Some* visibility has to be present for differences to be defined in racial terms, but that visibility is sometimes quite low. Thus the majority of German Jews before World War II was not physically identifiable as such. Yet the vast majority of Christians and many Jews defined Jews as a race. Conversion to Christianity, agnosticism, atheism, and full cultural assimilation in the dominant group did not remove the stigma of being a Jew. Although the visibility of Jews was so low that the Nazis imposed the wearing of stars of David, German anti-Semitism was clearly an example of racism rather than ethnocentrism, and German Jews did constitute a socially defined "race." The same situation applies to France, where Jews are also regarded by many as a race even though they are both highly acculturated and invisible, whereas highly visible and culturally distinct people of African origin are not [29].

Race relations, then, constitute a discrete class of phenomena, but only in a very limited way, that is, in the societal definition of group membership, in the criteria for prejudice and discrimination, and in the special folk theory of determination of behavior. Otherwise, race relations share the characteristics of other stratification systems, and race indeed often operates simultaneously with other criteria of invidious status differentiation. The greatest distinctiveness that we can attribute to race is that it is an *extreme case of status ascription making for rigid group membership*. Even as an extreme case, race is not unique. The traditional Hindu caste system, although it has been largely nonracial, at least in recent centuries, is nevertheless fully as ascribed, closed, and rigid as most multiracial societies. Moreover, status distinctions based on sex, which are found in all societies, rival race in their degree of rigidity and ascription.

Nevertheless, as a special, identifiable, and extreme instance of a more general social phenomenon, race deserves the attention it has received, because properly studied in the context of total societies it highlights social structures, processes, and conflicts in sharper form than other instances of social stratification. Race relations are an especially strategic vantage point for sociological analysis.

A Typology of Race Relations

Many scholars, such as Wirth, Cox, Simpson and Yinger, Wagley, Lieberson, and Merton and Frazier, have presented typologies of race relations, but their schemes have been of restricted use. These typologies have generally failed to relate race relations to the total society; some have been based on a single criterion such as aspirations of the subordinated group, policies of the dominant group, the indigenous or immigrant status of the dominant group, or the basis of group definition [30]. Others have been constructed around the interrelation of two dichotomous variables, using the device of the two-by-two table [31]. Others have been little more than *ad hoc* lists of situations without clarifying the variables along which the distinctions were made [32].

In an attempt to transcend the limitations of these approaches, I tried, by the Weberian ideal-type method, to arrive at a classification meeting the following criteria:

1. Comparative applicability, at least to the multiracial societies created by the expansion of Europe since the fifteenth century which together account for most of the world's racially stratified societies.
2. Historical usability in analyzing the evolution of race relations within a given society.
3. Specification of the dimensions or variables along which the typology is constructed.

4. Integration of the specific syndrome of race relations with the rest of the social structure.

Students of comparative race relations cannot but note basic similarities in social structure which transcend cultural differences. Thus, as rightly noted by Tannenbaum, the racial attitudes of the Spanish and Portuguese and the legal and religious status of slaves in Latin America were quite different from those in the English Colonies [33]. Overriding these differences were close similarities in structure between the slave plantations of northeastern Brazil and the ante-bellum southern United States. (Gilberto Freyre, in comparing these two slave regimes, used the phrase "latifundiary monoculture" to describe them [34].) Indeed, race relations in eighteenth-century Brazil resemble those in the ante-bellum southern United States more closely than the ante-bellum situation resembles contemporary United States race relations.

If two societies with widely different cultural traditions can more or less independently develop similar racial situations and institutions, if, conversely, the history of a given country can be marked by profound changes and discontinuities, and, furthermore, if abrupt qualitative changes in race relations can be shown to coincide with structural changes in the society at large, it is reasonable to accept that basic aspects of the social structure exert a considerable degree of determinism on the prevailing type of race relations. Such is the fundamental argument underlying the typology of race relations which I shall present shortly.

By stressing similarities between several societies of the same type, I do not reject, of course, the notion that important differences also exist between them, for indeed differences always exist between any two societies which have developed independently of one another. In other terms, *the factors or variables that we shall examine do not account for all of the variance in race relations.* My argument is simply that cultural idiosyncrasies specific to a given place and time, far from preventing cross-cultural uniformities and making generalizations impossible, leave a large residual of similarities unaccounted for except in terms of the broad economic and political infrastructure.

On the basis of this general formulation, I suggest that it is useful to analyze race relations in terms of two ideal types, which, for lack of better words, I have called "paternalistic" and "competitive" [35].

1. Race relations in a *paternalistic* system follow the master-servant model. The dominant group, often a small minority of less than ten per cent of the total population, rationalizes its rule in an ideology of benevolent despotism and regards members of the subordinate group as childish, immature, irresponsible, exuberant, improvident, fun-loving, good humored, and happy-go-lucky; in short, as inferior but lovable as long as they stay in "their place." In the subordinate group there is generally an ostensible accommodation to inferior status and sometimes even an internalization of inferiority feelings expressed through self-deprecation.

Roles and statuses are sharply defined along racial lines, with a rigidly ascriptive division of labor and a great asymmetry and complementarity in social relationships. Social distance between racial castes is maximized and symbolized by an elaborate and punctilious etiquette involving nonreciprocal terms of address, sumptuary regulations, and repeated manifestations of subservience and dominance. This great degree of social distance allows close symbiosis and even intimacy, without any threat to status inequalities. Consequently, physical segregation is not prominently used as a mechanism of social control and may, in fact, be totally absent between masters and servants living together in a state of "distant intimacy." Miscegenation in the form of institutionalized concubinage between women of the subordinate group and men of the dominant group is not only frequent but accepted by the ruling group as another of its legitimate prerogatives and forms of exploitation. The offspring of such unions is either assimilated to the subordinate group (often with a somewhat privileged status within it) or it develops into a distinct intermediate group. Racial prejudice on the part of the ruling group is, of course, present but seems to be related more directly to economic and social position than to any deep underlying psychodynamics. This prejudice often takes the form of "pseudo-tolerance" as exemplified by professions of love for the subordinate group as long as inequality is unchallenged. Genteel benevolence and *noblesse oblige* rather than virulent hatred characterize the paternalistic brand of bigotry. Open, collective aggression in a paternalistic system originates almost invariably from the subordinate group in the form of slave rebellions, and revivalistic, messianistic, or nationalistic movements.

A paternalistic type of race relations is characteristic of fairly complex but preindustrial societies, in which agriculture and handicraft production constitute the bases of the economy. Large-scale production of a cash-crop on slave plantations is a common and perhaps the "purest" case of paternalistic relations as shown by the pre-abolition regimes in northeastern Brazil, the Western Cape Province of South Africa, the West Indies, and the southern United States. Colonial regimes using various forms of forced labor, the *encomienda* system in Spanish America, and other types of land-based serfdom or indenture also exhibit many of the characteristics of paternalism.

Such societies are rigidly stratified into racial castes which are separated by a wide gulf in status, occupation, education, health standards, income, life style, and sometimes also in cultural tradi-tion. The class distinctions that may exist within castes are less important than the caste barrier, which is horizontal in the sense that there is no overlap in class status between castes. The color line allows no mobility except within castes, and even emancipa-tion in slavery systems often does not appreciably improve the freedman's status. Race is, with age and sex, the major criterion for the division of labor: manual work, whether in agriculture, domestic service, or handicraft, is the sole occupation open to members of the subordinate group or groups, and conversely supervisory, managerial, governmental, and professional func-tions are monopolized by the dominant caste. An elaborate ide-ology of racism and caste superiority buttresses such regimes, which, in relatively stable agrarian societies, can show great resilience and longevity. Conflict is, of course, present as in all social systems, but paternalistic regimes are based at least partly on the acquiescence of the subordinate group. Close face-to-face ties between masters and servants reinforce the status quo and supplement the use of coercion. Government in this type of social system tends to be vested in a feudal, land-owning aristocracy which often also owns, or at least closely controls, the labor force. Colonial or white settler bureaucracies are another type of paternalistic government. Paternalistic regimes are thus extreme examples of tyranny over, and exploitation of, the many by the few. The relative stability of these regimes is partly a product of coercion but, at least as importantly, of close, intimate, albeit highly unequal symbiosis. The very asymmetry and complementarity of economic ties between racial castes makes for a tightly integrated pattern of economic interdependence. In addition, miscegenation and other forms of unequal but intimate social relations create powerful affective (although often ambivalent) bonds across caste lines.

2. The *competitive* type of race relations represents the polar opposite of the paternalistic type. It is characteristic of industrialized and urbanized societies with a complex division of labor and a manufacturing basis of production. The dominant group is frequently a majority or a large minority (more than 20 or 25 per cent). There is still a color bar, and racial membership remains ascribed, but *class* differences become more salient relative to caste; that is, there is a greater range of class status within castes, whereas the gap in education, income, occupation, and living style between castes tends to narrow. Typically, there is even an overlap in class status between castes, so that the caste line is best described as oblique rather than horizontal [36]. Racial membership still plays a role in the division of labor, but achieved criteria of selection take precedence over strictly ascriptive ones. In a complex industrial economy that requires high skill levels the labor force has to be relatively free and mobile, and race is no longer workable as the paramount criterion for job selection; at least a heavy price in productivity has to be paid if racial ascription of occupations is to be retained. The political system often takes the form of a "*Herrenvolk* democracy," that is, a parliamentary regime in which the exercise of power and suffrage is restricted, *de facto,* and often *de jure,* to the dominant group.

In such a dynamic industrial society, with its great geographical mobility and its stress on impersonal market mechanisms and universalistic and achieved criteria of occupational selection, race relations are quite different from what they are under agrarian conditions. The master-servant model with its elaborate caste etiquette and its mechanisms of subservience and social distance breaks down to be replaced by acute competition between the subordinate caste and the working class within the dominant group. To the extent that social distance diminishes, physical segregation is introduced as a second line of defense for the preservation of the dominant group's position. The amount of contact between castes declines as the society becomes increasingly compartmentalized into racially homogeneous ghettoes with their nearly self-sufficient institutional structure. Miscegenation decreases in frequency and becomes more clandestine and stigmatized in both dominant and subordinate groups.

Given the more advanced state of industrialization characteristic of competitive societies, the division of labor makes for more "organic solidarity" and greater complementarity of roles than in a paternalistic system. However, role complementarity and asymmetry cut across racial cleavages in competitive societies. The racial cleavages no longer follow lines of economic interdependence but rather express themselves through spacial segregation at the ecological level and duplication of analogous institutions (e.g., in parallel church organizations and school systems) at the level of social structure. In other words, in a competitive system racial cleavages make for *segmentation without differentiation* and, in so doing, conflict with economic imperatives in a way that is not true of paternalistic systems in which caste lines combine the features of segmentation *and* differentiation. The growth of interdependence on lines other than racial ones and the structural and ecological fragmentation of competitive societies then pull in opposite directions and constitute one of the major sources of strain and disequilibrium in such systems.

The dominant group's image of the lower caste changes from one of backward but ingratiating grownup children to one of aggressive, insolent, "uppity," clannish, dishonest, underhanded competitors for scarce resources and challengers of the status quo. Virulent hatred replaces condescending benevolence and the psychopathology of bigotry finds a social outlet in scapegoating. Political consciousness develops in the oppressed group or groups; conflict is endemic and frequently erupts in both dominant and subordinate groups in the form of lynching, pogroms, race riots,

A Schematic Outline of the Paternalistic and the Competitive Types of Race Relations

A. "INDEPENDENT" VARIABLES*

	Paternalistic	Competitive
1. Economy	Nonmanufacturing, agricultural, pastoral, handicraft; mercantile capitalism; plantation economy	Typically manufacturing, but not necessarily so; large-scale industrial capitalism
2. Division of labor	Simple ("primitive") or intermediate (as in pre-industrial large-scale societies). Division of labor along racial lines. Wide income gap between racial groups	Complex (manufacturing) according to "rational" universalistic criteria; narrow gap in wages; no longer strictly racial
3. Mobility	Little mobility either vertical or horizontal (slaves, servants, or serfs "attached" in space)	Much mobility both vertical and horizontal (required by industrial economy)
4. Social stratification	Caste system with horizontal color bar; aristocracy versus servile caste with wide gap in living standards (as indexed by income, education, death and birth rates); homogeneous upper caste	Caste system but with tendency for color bar to "tilt" to vertical position; complex stratification into classes within castes; narrower gaps between castes and greater range within castes
5. Numerical ratio	Dominant group a small minority	Dominant group a majority
6. Value conflict	Integrated value system; no ideological conflict	Conflict at least in Western "Christian," "democratic," "liberal" type of society

* By "independent" variables I mean here those basic structural factors that determine to a large extent the prevailing type of race relations in a given society. By "dependent" variables, I mean more specifically aspects or components of the racial situation.

B. "DEPENDENT" VARIABLES*

	Paternalistic	Competitive
1. Race relations	Accommodation; everyone in "his place" and "knows it"; paternalism; benevolent despotism	Antagonism; suspicion, hatred; competitiveness (real or imaginary)
2. Roles and statuses	Sharply defined roles and statuses based on ascription, particularism, diffuseness, collectivity orientation, affectivity; unequal status unthreatened	Ill-defined and based on achievement, universalism, specificity, self-orientation, affective neutrality; unequal status threatened
3. Etiquette	Elaborate and definite	Simple and indefinite
4. Forms of aggression	Generally from lower caste: slave rebellions; nationalistic, revivalistic, or messianistic movements; not directly racial	Both from upper and lower caste; more frequent and directly racial: riots, lynchings, pogroms; passive resistance, sabotage, organized mass protests
5. Miscegenation	Condoned and frequent between upper caste males and lower caste females; institutionalized concubinage	Severely condemned and infrequent
6. Segregation	Little of it; status gap allows close but unequal contact	Much of it; narrowing of status gap makes for increase of spacial gap
7. Psychological syndrome	Internalized subservient status; no personality "need" for prejudice; no "high F"; "pseudo-tolerance"	"Need" for prejudice; "high F"; linked with sexuality, sadism, frustration; scapegoating
8. Stereotypes of lower caste	Childish, immature, exuberant, uninhibited, lazy, impulsive, fun-loving, good-humored; inferior but lovable	Aggressive, uppity, insolent, oversexed, dirty; inferior, despicable, and dangerous
9. Intensity of prejudice	Fairly constant	Variable and sensitive to provocative situations

C. "SOCIAL CONTROL" VARIABLES

	Paternalistic	Competitive
1. Form of govern- ment	Aristocratic, oligarchic, autocratic; either centra- lized or "feudal"; colonial	Restricted or pseudo- democratic
2. Legal system	Lower caste has definite legal status; law on side of racial *status quo*	Lower caste has no defi- nite legal status, resort to extra-legal sanctions (e.g., lynchings)

and terrorism as well as in disciplined mass movements of politi- cal opposition ranging from ordinary demonstrations to passive resistance. Situations exhibiting the characteristics of competitive race relations include modern United States, Britain, and South Africa, Eastern European anti-Semitism, and anti-Chinese or anti-Indian prejudice in such countries as Kenya, British Guiana, Malaya, and Indonesia.

It should be apparent that the typology of race relations just outlined closely parallels the well-known distinction in social science between *Gemeinschaft* and *Gesellschaft*. The scheme just outlined represents little more than an application and elabora- tion of this useful dichotomy to the field of race relations. The main variables that make up the social, economic, and political structure of a society are not only complexly interrelated but they determine to a considerable extent the type of race relations prevailing in that society at a given period in time. The formula- tion I have just sketched does meet the four conditions mentioned earlier: it specifies the factors that differentiate the two types; it relates the syndrome of race relations to the rest of the social structure; and it can be used both synchronically to compare societies and diachronically to study the evolution of a given society through time.

Thus, using the scheme, slave societies can be compared with one another and important similarities can become evident. Alternatively, by examining, say, the United States before and after the Civil War, we can relate changes in patterns of race relations meaningfully to more fundamental transformations in the economic, social, and political structure. To this type of analysis I shall turn presently. Naturally, given empirical cases seldom exhibit all the characteristics of an ideal type, which must be regarded as an analytical tool rather than as a shorthand description of a given situation. At best, one finds only approximations, and given instances typically show varying mixtures of the characteristics of both ideal types. For example, in the process of a society's evolution from a paternalistic to a competitive situation a number of "survivals" of the paternalistic type can linger on for long periods, even though the society as a whole clearly moves toward a closer approximation to competitive conditions; or, as in South Africa, governmental policies may endeavor to re-establish a paternalistic utopia in an acutely competitive situation. The principal task of the next four chapters is to illustrate the utility of this typology.

Race and the Theory of Pluralism and Conflict

Two important concepts, those of *pluralism* and *conflict,* are of great value in the analysis of multiracial societies. Pluralism is not used here in the limited sense in which American political and other social scientists in the de Tocquevillian tradition have, that is, in reference to competing and organized groups in a body politic whose overlapping and mutually canceling influence and interests contribute to a democratic balance of power. Here pluralism is used more broadly to refer to societies exhibiting to a greater or lesser degree two basic features. Societies are pluralistic insofar as they are *segmented into corporate groups* that frequently, although not necessarily, have different cultures or subcultures and insofar as their *social structure is compartmentalized into analogous, parallel, noncomplementary but distinguishable sets of institutions* [37]. These two defining criteria of pluralism (institutional duplication or multiplication as distinct from differentiation and cleavage between corporate groups) distinguish plural societies both from societies with segmentary kinship units (such as lineages, moieties, or clans) and from societies with a high degree of functional differentiation or specialization in their institutional structure. The segmentary, undifferentiated society characterized by what Durkheim called "mechanical solidarity" is, of course, divided into clearly defined corporate groups (typically unilineal descent groups), but it has a unitary, homogeneous institutional structure. On the other hand, the functionally differentiated society with "organic" solidarity has multiple but complementary and interrelated institutions [38]. Additional characteristics frequently associated with pluralism are the following:

1. Relative absence of value consensus.
2. Relative presence of cultural heterogeneity.
3. Relative presence of conflict between the significant corporate groups.
4. Relative autonomy between parts of the social system.
5. Relative importance of coercion and economic interdependence as bases of social integration.
6. Political domination by one of the corporate groups over the others.
7. Primacy of segmental, utilitarian, nonaffective, and functionally specific relationships *between* corporate groups, and of total, nonutilitarian, affective, diffuse ties *within* such groups. (In Cooley's terms, primary ties predominate *within* groups and secondary ties *between* groups.)

Clearly, pluralism is a matter of degree. Thus South Africa, which is divided into four major racial castes and into several unrelated cultural traditions represented by large proportions of its population, is more pluralistic than the United States which has only two major racial castes and shares, except for small minorities, the same Western culture and closely related dialects of the same language.

In light of these criteria, the segmentation and stratification of a society along racial lines constitute a special case of pluralism. It is useful here to distinguish between *cultural* and *social* pluralism. The first type results from the presence within a given society of several *ethnic* groups, or, at least in the minimum case, of several distinguishable varieties of the same cultural tradition (such as class-based subcultures). Social pluralism, however, is present in pure form to the extent that a society is structurally compartmentalized into analogous and duplicatory but culturally alike sets of institutions, and into corporate groups which are differentiated on a basis other than culture. In practice, social

and cultural pluralism often go together and can thus be regarded as two facets of the same phenomenon. The analytical
distinction, however, remains useful, for although cultural pluralism is almost invariably accompanied by social pluralism the
latter can be found in the nearly total absence of cultural
pluralism. Such is the case of the United States where rigid and
persistent racial cleavages (an important instance of social pluralism) have persisted in spite of relatively great cultural homo-
geneity. Even in societies where significant degrees of both
social and cultural pluralism exist, the lines of cleavage often
do not coincide; for example, in South Africa, a person may
culturally belong to the European group but be socially defined
as non-European by virtue of a racial criterion. The interplay
between race and culture, and between their corresponding forms
of pluralism, is of great importance in the analysis of racial
stratification as we shall see in Chapter 7.

The second important concept to be mentioned here, that of
conflict, has, of course, long preoccupied social scientists, but
among many American students of race relations there is a
curious reluctance to give it the central place it deserves. Many
functionalists have stressed consensus, harmony, equilibrium and
integration, and have regarded conflict almost as a dirty word.
Yet it should be obvious that the dimension of coercion versus
consent, or conflict versus accommodation, is basic to sociological
analysis in general and to race relations in particular. The recent
rehabilitation of conflict theory in social science, represented in
the works of authors such as Gluckman, Aguirre Beltrán, Dahrendorf, and Coser, is a healthy trend [39]. More specifically, the
Marxian conception that the dialectical opposition between
conflicting groups constitutes an important source of social
change can be usefully applied to the field of race relations. The
existing degree of conflict is one of the basic dimensions in which
the paternalistic type of race relations differs from the competitive one and the instability and change typical of the competitive
type result in large measure from the dialectic of conflict between
subordinate and dominant groups.

In Chapters 6 and 7 I shall return to some of the conceptual
problems raised in this Introduction. Meanwhile I shall try to

vindicate the utility of the approach I just sketched by applying these ideas to the analysis of four widely different case studies. For each of the four countries, I shall trace, however briefly, the evolution of race relations, stressing both similarities and differences. Because of space limitations, I cannot introduce much direct evidence and thus shall merely sketch the salient features of systems of race relations as they change through time [40].

Among the societies that evolved from European expansion since the sixteenth century, I have deliberately chosen instances that cover the entire spectrum from minimum to maximum salience of race as a criterion of group membership. Mexico is a limiting case of racial stratification, for group membership is predominantly determined by ethnic, class, and other nonphysical criteria. South Africa represents the other end of the spectrum with its rigid four-caste system. Brazil and the United States are located somewhere in between these two extremes, with Brazil falling closer to Mexico and the United States to South Africa. Yet I shall endeavor to show that important similarities of structure and historical evolution underlie the rather wide cultural differences between these countries.

NOTES

[1] Thomas F. Pettigrew, *A Profile of the Negro American,* pp. 100–135.

[2] Cf. A. Kardiner and L. Ovesey, *The Mark of Oppression.*

[3] The "null hypothesis," frequently used in statistics, consists in hypothesizing that there is no real difference (i.e., a difference not accountable for by "chance") between two samples or universes. If a difference is found (e.g., between mean scores) that could have occurred by chance only in one case in 20, 100, or 1000 (depending on the "confidence level" considered adequate), the null hypothesis is rejected. If, however, a difference is found that falls short of "statistical significance," we cannot accept the null hypothesis because we do not know whether the observed difference is a product of measurement errors, rounding errors, sample bias, or other "chance" factors or indeed whether it is "real." Beyond the smallest samples and the crudest measurements differences between any two groups are almost invariably present.

[4] See titles under these names in the bibliography.

[5] Cf. Gonzalo Aguirre Beltrán, *El Proceso de Aculturación.*

[6] The comparative work of Frank Tannenbaum in *Slave and Citizen,*

Oscar Handlin's *Race and Nationality in American Life,* John Hope Franklin's *From Slavery to Freedom* and C. Vann Woodward's *The Strange Career of Jim Crow* stand out as models of historiography in the field.

[7] Cf. bibliography.

[8] Gilberto Freyre, *The Masters and the Slaves.*

[9] Among the exceptions have been the works of Gonzalo Aguirre Beltrán, Gilberto Freyre, Marvin Harris, and Charles Wagley, who span history, anthropology, and sociology. Gordon W. Allport in his *Nature of Prejudice* probably goes furthest in trying to summarize the contributions of psychology and sociology, but he ends up with an eclectic acceptance of the various approaches as mutually complementary. He suggests by implication that an attempt at true theoretical synthesis across disciplinary boundaries may yet be premature.

[10] John Horton, "Order and Conflict Theories of Social Problems as Competing Ideologies."

[11] Gunnar Myrdal, *An American Dilemma.* O. C. Cox has attacked Myrdal's position in *Caste, Class and Race.*

[12] Mexican social scientists, who for the most part are the product of a revolutionary tradition, have taken the latter view, as exemplified by Gonzalo Aguirre Beltrán's statement in *El Proceso de Aculturación.* This is also the perspective I have adopted in my *South Africa, A Study in Conflict.*

[13] In Appendix 2 of that book Myrdal devotes about thirty pages to problems of objectivity in social science and in the field of race relations.

[14] Cf. George E. Simpson and J. Milton Yinger, *Racial and Cultural Minorities,* pp. 30–33; M. F. Ashley Montagu, *Introduction to Physical Anthropology;* and Stanley M. Gann and Carleton S. Coon, "On the Number of Races of Mankind."

[15] See Warner's introduction to Allison W. Davis, B. B. Gardner, and M. R. Gardner, *Deep South.*

[16] Cf. O. C. Cox, *Caste, Class and Race.*

[17] In spite of the narrower connotation which the word "racism" has acquired for many people, my usage is congruent with the definition of the term in the Webster dictionary: "Assumption of inherent racial superiority or the purity and superiority of certain races, and consequent discrimination against other races; also any doctrine or program of racial domination and discrimination based on such an assumption. Also less specif., race hatred and discrimination."

[18] M. G. Smith, *The Plural Society in the British West Indies,* p. 132.

[19] Cf. Richard Hofstadter, *Social Darwinism in American Thought.*

[20] I dealt with this concept of *Herrenvolk* democracy and egalitarianism in my book, *South Africa, A Study in Conflict.*

[21] Gordon W. Allport, *The Nature of Prejudice,* remains the best and least dogmatic summary of the field from a social-psychological perspective. Other textbooks by sociologists also devote much space to the contributions of social psychologists. Such is the case, for example,

of George E. Simpson and J. Milton Yinger, *Racial and Cultural Minorities.*

[22] A good recent survey of the literature on the Negro American can be found in Thomas F. Pettigrew, *A Profile of the Negro American.*

[23] For a good critique of the "frustration-aggression" theory, see Gordon W. Allport, *op. cit.*, Chapter 21. See also John Dollard et al., *Frustration and Aggression.*

[24] Cf. T. W. Adorno et al., *The Authoritarian Personality.* For critiques of that study, see Richard Christie and Marie Jahoda, eds., *Studies in the Scope and Method of "The Authoritarian Personality."* The "F" stands for Fascism, and the "E" for ethnocentrism in the designation of the scales used by Adorno and his colleagues.

[25] Robert K. Merton deals with the dissociation of racial attitudes and behavior in "Discrimination and the American Creed."

[26] Thomas F. Pettigrew, *Regional Differences in Anti-Negro Prejudice.*

[27] See, for example, Lewis M. Killian's article in Raymond M. Mack, ed., *Race, Class and Power.*

[28] The process of "decolonization" in recent African history illustrates how rapidly Europeans adjusted both their attitudes and their behavior toward black Africans. Of course, some whites did not adjust and left after independence, and others modified their behavior but not their attitudes, but many, if not most, whites showed remarkable adaptation to drastically changed political and social conditions. Unfortunately, this process of attitude change has not been extensively studied, and these assertions are based mostly on "impressionistic" evidence. For more solid evidence of anticipatory adaptation to "Africanization" by colonial whites in Northern Rhodesia, see J. F. Holleman, J. W. Mann, and Pierre L. van den Berghe, "A Rhodesian White Minority under Threat." In a reverse situation which I personally observed in 1948 during a three-week sea voyage from Antwerp, Belgium, to Lobito, Angola, approximately half of the passengers were old colonials returning to the Congo, whereas the other half were Belgians on their first trip to Africa. The catering personnel of the ship consisted exclusively of Congolese men. During the first days of the crossing, the "new" colonials, unfamiliar with the sight of African waiters and cabin attendants, behaved toward them with greater politeness and formality than they would have toward whites in the same situation, addressing them as "Monsieur," for example. Within a week or so, many of the "new" colonials had adapted their behavior to that of the "old" colonials who "knew how to handle the natives." By the end of the crossing, many of the new colonials had developed a full set of anti-African stereotypes and racist attitudes, and outdid, for the most part, the "old" colonials in their discourtesy to the African personnel. The same persons who two or three weeks earlier had called Africans "Monsieur" were now hurling epithets such as *macaque* (rhesus monkey) at them. This was particularly true of the less educated Belgians.

[29] For a perceptive study of French Jewry see Pierre Aubery, *Milieux*

Juifs de la France Contemporaine. Aubery documents well the nearly complete acculturation of French Jews, although he tends to underestimate the amount of anti-Semitism.

[30] Stanley Lieberson, "A Societal Theory of Race and Ethnic Relations"; George E. Simpson and J. Milton Yinger, *op. cit.,* pp. 25–32; Louis Wirth, "The Problem of Minority Groups," pp. 354–363.

[31] Robert K. Merton, *op. cit.,* pp. 103–110.

[32] O. C. Cox, *op. cit.,* pp. 353–354; E. Franklin Frazier, *Race and Culture Contacts in the Modern World,* pp. 11–36. In addition to the typologies of race and ethnic relations alluded to here, several other sociological approaches have been used. For example, W. Lloyd Warner analyzed Negro-White relations in terms of stratification into castes which are themselves divided into classes; this schema was also adopted by Gunnar Myrdal, John Dollard, Allison W. Davis, B. B. Gardner, M. R. Gardner, and others. This "school" has been under fire from Marxist scholars like O. C. Cox who stress that "race" is an aspect of class struggle in capitalist societies. Another influential "school" has been that represented by Robert E. Park and his students at Chicago who held that race and ethnic relations went through a four-phase cycle of contact, competition, accommodation, and assimilation. Anthropologists like Melville J. Herskovits and Robert Redfield stressed the dynamics of acculturation as the main factor influencing intergroup relations. Finally, a wide range of psychological theories ranging from behaviorism to psychoanalysis has been applied to the study of racial and ethnic attitudes. A detailed critique of these approaches would be redundant, since extensive treatments of the existing theoretical literature can be found in several good textbooks. See for example, Gordon W. Allport, *The Nature of Prejudice;* George E. Simpson and J. Milton Yinger, *Racial and Cultural Minorities;* and James W. Vander Zanden, *American Minority Relations.*

[33] Frank Tannenbaum, *Slave and Citizen.*

[34] Cf. *The Masters and the Slaves.*

[35] An early version of the typology appeared in my article, "The Dynamics of Racial Prejudice." A more extended statement can be found in my paper, "Paternalistic versus Competitive Race Relations." A schematic outline of the typology can be found on pp. 31–33.

[36] See W. Lloyd Warner's classic formulation of the "caste and class" system of the United States in his introduction to Allison W. Davis, B. B. Gardner, and M. R. Gardner, *Deep South.*

[37] My usage of the concept of pluralism is broadly congruent with that developed in recent years by British or British-trained social anthropologists and sociologists who have worked in Africa or the West Indies. See the works of M. G. Smith, Leo Kuper, Elena Padilla, J. Clyde Mitchell, and Philip Mayer in the bibliography. In my article "Toward a Sociology of Africa" and the final chapter of my book, *South Africa, A Study in Conflict,* I have expanded on the concept of pluralism. Coming from a different tradition, Gonzalo Aguirre Beltrán

independently developed in the Mexican context an analytical framework which has many points of convergence with the works just cited. See his *El Proceso de Aculturación*. For a different use of the concept of pluralism in the context of United States race relations, see Milton M. Gordon, *Assimilation in American Life*. The apparent contradiction between the two traditions in the use of the concept of pluralism will concern us again at the end of the final chapter of this book.

[38] Cf. Emile Durkheim, *The Division of Labor in Society*.

[39] See their works in the bibliography.

[40] For supplementary material, the reader is referred to the classified bibliography by country. If works are primarily comparative or stress general theory, they are listed in the first section of the bibliography even though they may also deal specifically with one of four countries chosen as case studies in this book.

II

Mexico

Of all the multiracial societies created by the expansion of Europe since the late fifteenth century, those of Spanish America stand out as exhibiting only traces of the racist virus. Indeed, most of these countries constitute such limiting cases that one may more properly speak of ethnic relations. This is true not only in predominantly "white" countries such as Argentina, Chile, and Uruguay but also in Bolivia, Ecuador, Peru, and Guatemala where Indians still comprise 40 to 45 per cent of the population, in Venezuela and Cuba with their strong African admixtures, and in other Spanish-speaking countries where mestizos dominate the scene. To this last category belongs Mexico where the very term *mestizo,* originally a racial one used to designate the mixture of European and Indian, has now acquired a cultural meaning, and is applied to practically anybody who is not of recent European origin and who speaks the Mexican dialect of Spanish as his mother tongue. Over 85 per cent of today's population of the Republic fall in that category.

Racial characteristics have so little social relevance in modern Mexico and the complex interplay of race and culture through the dual process of miscegenation and hispanization have so homogenized the Mexican population that race and ethnic relations in that country have received scant attention from social scientists. To these factors making for the scarcity of studies in

42

that area must be added the official (and largely justified) denial that Mexico has any "racial problem" and the Revolutionary ideology extolling Mexico as a "nation of bronze," a harmonious alloy of the Old and the New World. Scholars from north of the Rio Grande, comparing Mexico with their own country, have readily accepted that thesis. The task of providing us with an integrated and balanced account of race and ethnic relations in Mexico since the Conquest has been performed mostly by a prominent intellectual product of the Mexican Revolution, the anthropologist Gonzalo Aguirre Beltrán [1].

The origins of modern Mexico go back to the Spanish Conquest of 1519 to 1523, the extraordinary brutality and treachery of which is attested to by the candid eye-witness account of Bernal Díaz del Castillo [2]. Aided by an unusual set of circumstances (such as the initial belief that Cortés had fulfilled by his coming the prophecy of the return of Quetzalcoatl), by their horses and firearms, and by their readiness to resort to terror and duplicity, a few hundred Spaniards destroyed the powerful Aztec empire and established within a decade their domination over most of present Mexico. Until the Mexican War of Independence of the 1810s the North American possessions of the Spanish Crown became known as the Vice-Royalty of New Spain and were ruled as a colony from Madrid. Every attempt was made forcibly to convert Indians to Catholicism, to destroy indigenous beliefs and practices (such as polygyny), and generally to impose the norms and values and to secure the political and economic interests of the conqueror.

In this process of forced "deculturation," indigenous societies were beheaded of their ruling and priestly class; the system of agriculture based on communal land exploitation by localized clans (*calpul*) was undermined; the Indians were forcibly relocated and reduced to serfdom through the *encomienda, repartimiento,* and debt peonage systems; and a quasi-feudal regime was established. The Indian population declined from an estimated 4.5 million in 1519 to 3.3 million in 1570 to 1.3 million in 1646 as a result of smallpox and typhus epidemics, wars, forced labor, and mistreatment on mines and plantations, heavy tribute demands, spoliation of land, and the general social and economic disruption which came in the wake of the Conquest [3].

For a short time after the Conquest the Spanish colonial government found it convenient to rule through the old Indian elite (whom they called *caciques* or "chiefs") at the local level, and occasionally a member of the Indian elite who converted to Catholicism was elevated to the Spanish nobility and co-opted into the ruling Spanish aristocracy. Generally, however, the Spaniards arrogated to themselves all important political, military, and religious offices, and established a system of stratification which, although not based strictly on race, was nevertheless rigid, at least in theory.

After a relatively short period of stabilization and consolidation of Spanish rule, the colony developed a quasi-feudal social structure which, although far from static, retained many of its basic elements until the Revolution of 1910 to 1917. The economic basis of New Spain was the exploitation, by means of servile labor and for the benefit of the Crown and the Spanish settlers, of the country's mineral and agricultural resources. Spain imposed rigidly mercantilistic restrictions on both external and internal trade, limiting the external trade to direct commerce between herself and her colonies and insuring the economic interests of the European settlers in internal trade. The commerce of imported goods and of some indigenous products such as cocoa was restricted to Spaniards. Access to artisan guilds and to administrative or military posts was similarly closed to Indians, mestizos, and Negroes (though exceptions were made in the late colonial period). Mining and agricultural production was under the almost exclusive control of the Spanish settlers. The Spanish Crown, through its policy of granting to individual Spanish settlers, as well as to convents and religious orders, the right to collect tribute in goods and services from the population living on given land estates, completely disrupted the native economy and reduced the Indian masses to symbiotic serfdom and dependence. This was the essence of the *encomienda* and *repartimiento* systems. These, in combination with debt peonage which assumed vast proportions in the eighteenth century and lasted until the Revolution, led to the development of Mexico's vast land estates (*haciendas*). In addition, under a policy of forced relocation, the Spanish Crown concentrated the Indian population in Spanish-type towns (*congregaciones*) with communally held land, thereby giving rise to a kind of reservation system. Some Indian groups sought refuge in the more remote areas (such as the highlands of Chiapas), where they managed partly to escape Spanish control and to maintain their ethnic identity to the present, but the majority of the Indian and mestizo population became landless *peones* or lived on the economic margin of the country in the Indian reservations.

This exploitative contact was accompanied by two continuing processes that dominated Mexican history: (a) hispanization, that is, the partly coerced, partly voluntary adoption of the colonial version of Spanish culture by the indigenous and African population; and (b) mestizoization, that is, the genetic mixture of the three main human stocks present in New Spain, the African, the European, and the Indian. Culturally, of course, modern Mexico is a mixture of indigenous and nonindigenous elements, but the Spanish component is clearly dominant. Biologically, the reverse is true; the Indian contribution to the national gene pool continues to dominate. At no time did the combined "pure" European and "pure" Negro African population in Mexico exceed 3 per cent of the total. "Pure" Indians declined from 98.7 per cent of the total in 1570 to 74.6 per cent in 1646, to 60.0 per cent in 1810, to 29.2 per cent in 1921 (the year of the last racial census), and to an estimated 20.0 per cent in 1950. The mestizos increased correspondingly to something like four fifths of the modern Mexican population. If the important cultural criterion of language is applied, however, no more than 10 to 11 per cent of the Mexican population still speak indigenous languages and that percentage has declined from 15.3 in 1900 to 10.4 in 1960 (see Table 2.2). In 1930, somewhat more than half the Indian population (53 per cent) spoke only Indian tongues; by 1950 two thirds (67 per cent) had become bilingual, that is, spoke at least limited Spanish [4]. Clearly, many people of pure or predominantly Indian stock have become more or less completely hispanicized, so much so that the racial definition of mestizo or Indian has now lost its meaning. Even the monolingual Indian enclaves are culturally quite different from the pre-Columbian Indian groups. They have become at least nominally Catholic and exhibit much syncretism of Spanish and preconquest cultures and religions [5].

Colonial New Spain, from the early seventeenth century to independence, was stratified into five distinct groups called *castas.* They were defined by a mixture of racial and cultural character- istics and could more accurately be described as estates rather than castes. The processes of hispanization and miscegenation increasingly blurred the dividing lines and made for considerable upward mobility (though for much less than in an open class system). The five *castas* were the following in decreasing order of status:

1. The *European Spaniards,* that is, those who came directly from Spain and were presumably pure white (though Sevilla in Andalusia was an important slave-trading center and thus not free of racial intermixture). This *casta,* which fluctuated from 0.2 to 0.8 per cent of the colonial population (see Table 2.1), nearly monopolized the higher civil, military, and religious posi- tions in the vice-regal government. It also owned a vastly dis- proportionate share of the land and of the servile population. The great majority being males, they intermixed with females of the other four *castas.* Concubinage accounted for most of the miscegenation, but isolated cases of intermarriage with Indians, mestizos, and even Negroes did occur. The Church favored inter- marriage over concubinage for religious and moral reasons; how- ever, interracial marriages were clearly regarded as *mésalliances* by the Spanish laity who, at the same time, condoned interracial concubinage between Spanish men and women of lower status, even in its multiple form. These attitudes were congruent with the traditional dual standard of Spanish sexual morality.

2. The *American Spaniards,* also known as *criollos* (creoles), were the completely hispanicized people born in the New World. They were regarded as whites and a few of them no doubt were, but most were descended from mestizos who had been recognized by their Spanish fathers and brought up as Spaniards. Over time, the tendency for European Spaniards to seek spouses in this group led to a gradual "bleaching" of the creoles, who thus became for the most part light mestizos. The creoles rapidly ex- panded through natural increase as well as "passing" from the lower groups. In 1570 they constituted a mere 0.3 per cent of the total; by 1646 they approached 10 per cent; at the close of Spanish rule they comprised nearly 18 per cent of the total (see

TABLE 2.1

Population of New Spain by "Castas" [6]

Year	Total	Europeans	Africans	Indians	Creoles	Afro-mestizos	Indo-mestizos
				Numbers			
1570	3,380,012	6,644	20,569	3,336,860	11,067	2,437	2,435
1646	1,712,615	13,780	35,089	1,269,607	168,568	116,529	109,042
1742	2,477,277	9,814	20,131	1,540,256	391,512	266,196	249,368
1793	3,799,561	7,904	6,100	2,319,741	677,458	369,790	418,568
1810	6,122,354	15,000	10,000	3,676,281	1,092,367	624,461	704,245
				Percentages			
1570	100.0	0.2	0.6	98.7	0.3	0.1	0.1
1646	100.0	0.8	2.0	74.6	9.8	6.8	6.0
1742	100.0	0.4	0.8	62.2	15.8	10.8	10.0
1793	100.0	0.2	0.1	61.0	17.8	9.7	11.2
1810	100.0	0.2	0.2	60.0	17.9	10.2	11.5

47

TABLE 2.2
Mexican Population over Five Years of Age Who Speak
an Indigenous Language as Mother Tongue

Date	Percentage of Total Population over Five	Number (in millions)
1900	15.3	1.78
1910	12.9	1.68
1920	15.2	1.89
1930	16.0	2.25
1940	14.8	2.49
1950	11.2	2.45
1960	10.4	3.03

Table 2.1). The creoles owned most of the land not in possession of the European Spaniards, they monopolized much of commerce and craft production, and they occupied the lesser offices in the colonial bureaucracy. They soon constituted a nascent bourgeoisie next to the aristocratic European Spaniards. The creoles like the European Spaniards were disproportionately represented in the urban centers, although they were sometimes landlords of large *haciendas*. On rare occasions a creole was appointed to a high office such as that of viceroy or bishop.

On the surface it might seem that the primary criterion for distinguishing the creoles from the other Spaniards was one of racial purity. But although such phrases as "purity" or "cleanliness of blood" testify to a mild form of racism among the Spaniards, the creoles were regarded more as provincials or colonials whose *cultural* purity had been corrupted by contact with superstitious heathens and who spoke an unrefined dialect of New World Spanish. The distinction between the two groups was thus at least as much cultural as racial.

The creoles nearly always married either endogamously or hypergamously with European Spaniards; they also engaged in extensive concubinage with the lower three groups, and in the process blurred the distinction between themselves and the mestizos.

3. *Mestizos* came next in descending order of prestige and privileges. They were the illegitimate products of unions between

Spaniards and Indians and between Indians and Negroes, as well as of the second and third generation mixtures between mestizos and the other nonwhite groups. In the melting pot of New Spain the mestizos came to constitute a residual category, which included anyone who did not belong to the other four estates. Within that group which steadily grew from 0.1 per cent in 1570, to 12.8 per cent in 1646, to 21.6 per cent in 1810, to about 85.0 per cent today, internal distinctions were made, but they became obsolete by the time of Independence. Concern for physical appearance gave rise to an elaborate nomenclature based on skin color, hair texture, and facial features. Afro-mestizos were sometimes distinguished from Indian-white mixtures by the term *zambaigo*. Finer distinctions of shades of pigmentation and types of crossing between Indians and whites gave rise to such terms as *mestizo blanco, castizo, mestizo prieto, mestizo pardo,* and *mestindio.*

Although this complex terminology was obviously the result of concern for racial appearance, the very minuteness of the distinctions militated in fact against the formation of rigid lines and facilitated "passing" and racial "upgrading." Thus Afro-mestizos tried to pass for Indians or Indian-white mestizos, for Indian "blood" was regarded as superior to Negro "blood," and by the early nineteenth century the very distinction between Afro- and Indo-mestizo had lost its meaning. Similarly, the *mulato blanco* and the *castizo* could often pass for creoles and sometimes did so by fraudulently changing the baptismal records which, as a rule, recorded the *casta*. By the late eighteenth century passing had become common enough to blur the difference between creoles and mestizos and to make the *casta* system fairly nominal.

Mestizos were technically debarred from most nonmanual occupations, but eventually these restrictions were less stringently applied. At first many mestizos were brought up by their mothers as Indians, but they became increasingly hispanicized to the point of being culturally indistinguishable from the creoles and European Spaniards. Unlike Indians and Negroes, mestizos were exempt from payment of the capitation tax, but their economic position was often little better.

4. *Indians* formed the broadest stratum of the colonial labor

force, namely the servile peasantry, the mass of the *peones* living on the *haciendas*. During the first decades after the Conquest the Spaniards distinguished between the indigenous nobility and the commoners, but the shock and disruption of Spanish rule homogenized Indian society to the lowly status of conquered helots. Forced to pay the capitation tax and to work on Spanish-owned farms and mines, displaced from their land to make room for large cattle farms, the Indians were ruthlessly exploited, reduced to destitution, and decimated by epidemic diseases against which they had built no immunity. Early attempts by the conquistadores and Spanish settlers to reduce Indians to outright slavery were thwarted by the pro-Indian representations of Bartolomé de las Casas, Bishop of Chiapas, to the Spanish Crown, and by the mid-sixteenth century Indian slavery was decreed out of existence.

Indians were officially granted the status of rational beings, of members of the human species, and serfdom was undoubtedly a lesser evil than slavery, but the lot of the Indian was certainly far from enviable. However, the Spaniards regarded themselves as superior to Indians not so much by virtue of race as of culture, and particularly of religion. They regarded Indians as pagans or as "new Christians" still addicted to superstitious and devilish practices and unable to speak the noble Castilian tongue.

The mass of Indians and, over time, more and more mestizos lived as *peones* on the large self-sufficient estates known as *haciendas*. The buildings, often surrounded by a walled enclosure, included the "big house" (*casa grande*), lodgings for peasants, workshops, stables, chapel, storerooms, jail, cemetery, and other dependencies. The owner had nearly absolute power over his serfs, who in the feudal manner had to pledge their loyalty and furnish tribute and labor in exchange for the right to live on the estate. The master-serf relationship was thus basic in uniting Spaniards and Indians in an exploitative symbiosis. The four main categories of *peones* were: the *arrendatario* or tenant, the *aparcero* or share-cropper, the *baldillo* who was obligated to furnish a certain number of days of labor, and the *peon acasillado* or agricultural wage laborer.

Little racial segregation existed on the *haciendas,* but an elaborate etiquette of subservience and respect as well as ties of ritual kinship (*compadrazgo*) maintained social distance while creating bonds of dependency between master and serf. Sumptuary regulations forbade Indians to wear Spanish clothes, to ride on horseback, and to use the title of *Don*.

The Spaniards generally preferred to live in their town houses rather than on the isolated *haciendas,* the management of which they often left to a mestizo or creole. Thus there emerged the pattern of the town occupied by Spaniards, creoles, and mestizos, serving as a center of commerce and handicraft production and living from the tribute and produce of the satellite rural Indian population. Some Indians who helped the early settlers build the towns acquired the privileged status of *villanos* (free townsmen) and quickly intermixed with Spaniards to give rise to the urban mestizo population from which the petty bourgeoisie developed.

5. At the lowest level of the colonial hierarchy were the *Negro and mulatto slaves.* The African contribution to the Mexican population is generally underrated. In the sixteenth and seventeenth centuries substantial numbers of slaves were imported through Veracruz and Acapulco and were scattered throughout New Spain, with a greater concentration in Mexico City and in the hot coastal regions. Not all slaves were Negroes. The Spaniards and Portuguese introduced Moorish and Berber slaves captured in the religious wars in Morocco and the Iberian Peninsula; the famous galleon traveling between Manila and Acapulco brought as part of its cargo slaves from Indonesia and the Asian mainland. However, the colonial government regarded white slaves as undesirable, not so much because they were white, but rather because it was feared that being Muslims they would proselyte among the Indians. The development of the African slave trade, first by the Portuguese and later by the Dutch, French, Danes, and English, soon made the overwhelming majority of Mexican slaves Negroes, mostly from West Africa, Angola, and Mozambique.

Until the mid-eighteenth century slaves outnumbered the Spaniards by two or three to one. Then a rapid decline in Mexican slavery began, largely as a consequence of competition from the rapidly growing, impoverished, and roving mestizo population. Slave labor was simply priced out of the market by free mestizo labor and by Indian serfs.

Negroes were introduced in the proportion of two men to every woman. Negro women were sexually exploited as concubines by their masters and gave rise to a mulatto group, some of whom found their way into the creole population after two generations of miscegenation. Negro men for the most part had relations with Indian women and gave rise to a large class of Afro-mestizos who constituted up to 10.8 per cent of the total population. In the long run, however, mulattoes and Negroes, because of the contempt in which they were held and the disabilities under which they suffered, sought to become assimilated with the Indians and mestizos and were so successful that most Mexicans today have forgotten the African contribution to their country's heritage.

An elaborate terminology was applied to various mixtures of Negroes with Indians and Spaniards and to the resulting shades in skin color and differences in other physical traits. *Mulato claro, mulato blanco, mulato prieto, mulato pardo, coyote, mulato lobo, mulato alobado, zambaigo, moreno, pardo, negro retinto,* and *negro amulatado* were among the more common terms used. They reveal both racial consciousness and the deprecation in which Negroes and mulattoes were held. Several of these words are names of animals and, of course, the term *mulato* itself is derived from mule, implying a cross between different biological species.

If the Spaniards exhibited a clear form of racism it was toward people of African descent. Indians were considered not as noble as the Spaniards to be sure, but neither were they considered intrinsically ignoble. They were in need of enlightenment through exposure to the true faith, but they were basically human. Spanish attitudes toward Negroes were distinctly different. Africans were regarded as a vile, immoral race possessing unclean blood and low intelligence. At the same time they were considered to have great muscular strength and endurance, manual dexterity and high fertility. These stereotypes were contrasted with those of the supposedly weak but more intelligent Indian. More specific stereotypes were ascribed to various ethnic groups from which African slaves were drawn.

In spite of these highly derogatory attitudes toward Negroes and mulattoes, slavery in Mexico was less brutal than in the English colonies, largely as a result of the tempering influence of the Catholic Church. Most notably, the Church, by favoring monogamous marriage and attempting to prevent the separation of married slaves made possible at least some degree of stable family life among Negroes.

As suggested before, such rigidity as this colonial *casta* system possessed was being undermined during the eighteenth century by increasing mestizoization and hispanization, the slow economic demise of slavery, and the absorption of the Negroes and mulattoes into the Indian and mestizo population. The War of Independence, much like the American Revolution, did not profoundly affect the economic and social structure of Mexico. The creoles, who were themselves in the process of becoming fused with the mestizos, supplanted the European Spaniards as a ruling class, and thus substituted an American-born aristocracy for a European regime. The gradual physical and cultural homogenization which had begun in the sixteenth century was perhaps slightly accelerated through political independence. A number of mestizos became prominent (e.g., one of the great independence heroes, Morelos, was an Afro-mestizo) and Mexicans gradually came to think of themselves as a mestizo nation. However, the economic and social infrastructure of the country, particularly the quasi-feudal *hacienda* system, was left unshaken.

The next wave of political change in Mexican history came with the *Reforma* under the leadership of Benito Juarez, a hispanicized Zapotec Indian. The *Reforma* was Mexico's "bourgeois revolution" and was modeled on European *laissez faire* liberalism with the added element of French-inspired anticlericalism. It marked the ascendancy of the urban mestizo bourgeoisie *vis à vis* the creole landed aristocracy, but it did not destroy the latter class. The major achievement of the *Reforma* was the introduction of separation between church and state and the consequent secularization of life and reduction in the power of the Church. The bourgeoisie, in conjunction with the landed aristocracy, the army, and foreign capital, reached the peak of its power during the Porfirio Diaz dictatorship which was overthrown in 1910 by the first true modern socialist revolution in Mexican history (and indeed one of the first in world history if we exclude the abortive Paris Commune).

The Revolution was a grass-root peasant revolt led by the urban intelligentsia and it established one of the first of the nationalist, left-leaning, anti-clerical, anti-imperialist, and anti-capitalist regimes which now characterize most of the Third World. The presently ruling *Partido Revolucionario Institucional* is the heir of the Mexican Revolution which liquidated the temporal involvement of the Church (in both its political and economic forms) in national affairs, introduced land reform by abolishing large absentee ownership and substituting the unique *ejido* system, and launched an enlightened policy of rehabilitation and guided assimilation of the remaining Indian minorities into the national population. The official ideology is militantly anti-racist, as shown, for instance, by the inspiration and presentation of the new National Museum of Anthropology in Mexico City. (For example, an inscription proclaims: ". . . all men have the same capacity to face nature . . . all races are equal . . . all cultures are worthy of respect, and . . . all peoples can live in peace.")

This recent period in Mexican history saw the virtual disappearance of the feudal model of agricultural production and of the master-servant relationship between the creole landowner and the Indian or mestizo peon. To be sure, in the more remote parts of the Republic (such as the Highlands of Chiapas), a system of exploitative interdependence between rural Indians and urban *ladinos* (as the local hispanicized mestizos are known) still exhibits many characteristics of the colonial period [7]. There the old paternalistic master-servant model of political subordination, economic exploitation, and social subservience still prevails, with a distinct etiquette of ethnic relations, the remnants of sumptuary regulations—a complex network of interethnic ritual kinship and stereotypes of the Indian as a simple-minded, inept, irresponsible, grownup child. (Indians are often referred to by *ladinos* in the diminutive form *indito,* which literally means "little Indian.") Even there, however, through the intervention of the *Instituto Nacional Indigenista* and gradual economic and political integration with the rest of the country, this quasi-feudal situation is breaking down.

We have briefly surveyed the social evolution of Mexico from a largely ascriptive system of ethno-racial estates exhibiting most of the characteristics of a paternalistic type of relations to an open class system in which the focus of group conflict and differences has shifted from ethnicity and race to social strata based on education, occupation, wealth, power, and prestige. The concept of race has become almost totally alien to modern Mexican culture; for every Mexican who takes pride in being of pure European ancestry there are at least two who indulge in the reverse snobbery of claiming to be pure Indian and ten who are proud of being mestizos. Even in these instances the claim to purity is often to be understood in a cultural context. Of course, the ethnocentric belief in the superiority of Spanish over Indian culture is still quite widespread, but among intellectuals this ethnocentrism has given rise to two main counter-ideologies: romantic Indianism with the exaltation of pre-Colombian civilizations and *indigenismo* or the stress on the actuality and desirability of cultural syncretism, and on the creation of an integrated mestizo nation.

Ethnicity is still an important factor in the remaining islands of Indian culture as mentioned earlier, and residual racism (often intertwined with ethnic prejudice) is still traceable in the folklore (proverbs, tales, and the like). A fairly widespread esthetic preference exists for light skin color, and blond hair and blue eyes are prized in women, if only because of their scarcity. Some correlation between phenotype and class status also remains; European-looking Mexicans are disproportionately represented in the upper and middle classes; however, dark mestizos and Indians are found in significant numbers at all class levels. Although there probably is some slight residual tendency toward racial homogamy, physical appearance is not an appreciable factor in social mobility or, more generally, in social behavior. Most Mexicans express sincere distaste and lack of understanding for racism, regarding it as a queer Yankee set of beliefs. With the massive influx of tourists from the United States since World War II, however, isolated incidents of "secondary racism" appear in hotels and restaurants; their managers occasionally discriminate against American Negroes in deference to the bigotry of their other Anglo-American guests.

Mexico can be described as having evolved from a paternalistic type of race and ethnic relations to a nonracial system without having gone through a competitive phase. In other words, race ceased to be a meaningful social reality and ethnicity was relegated to a residual position as the quasi-feudal colonial society broke down and gave rise to a modern class society. How did the concept of race fade out of Mexican social reality?

A common answer to this question is that racism never really existed in Mexico because it was alien to Spanish culture. It is true that Iberian racism was milder and quite different from the crude Northern European nineteenth-century variety of the phenomenon. Indeed, in Spain and Portugal the indigenous population had been ruled until the fifteenth century by the Moors who were both darker skinned and more educated than the natives. Hence, the Spaniards in the Old World did not associate dark skin with political or cultural inferiority; to say, however, that racism was unknown in Iberian culture, particularly in the New World, is an untenable overstatement. Physical traits were used to categorize people in colonial times; the elaborate racial terminology is symptomatic enough of concern for race; in addition, the frequent use of such phrases as "pure race," "clean blood," and "suspicious color" in colonial documents testify to the existence of Iberian racism. Having thus established the historical existence of the phenomenon, how can we account for its subsequent disappearance?

Several lines of explanation suggest themselves. First, the Spaniards seldom made a clear analytical distinction between race and culture. Rather, they tended to assume that the two went together, and their alleged cultural superiority has always been a greater source of pride to them than the "purity" of their physical makeup. The definition of the colonial *castas* was an inextricable mixture of ethnic and racial criteria and the latter predominated only in reference to the lowest group (Negroes and mulattoes).

Second, few of the invidious distinctions and discriminations prevailing during colonial times followed a strictly racial line. To virtually all rules, norms, and *casta*-linked disabilities there were important exceptions. There are, for example, recorded cases of intermarriage between Spaniards and both Indians and Negroes, and interracial marriage was never prohibited in Mexico. (For a brief period it was forbidden in Cuba, but the edict was rescinded within a few years.) Creoles occupied high offices, and a descendant of Moctezuma even rose to the Vice-Royalty. Full-blooded Indians were occasionally conferred Spanish titles of nobility. By the eighteenth century numerous exceptions were made to the technical exclusion of mestizos and mulattoes from artisanal guilds and civil and military positions. Laxity often prevailed in recording a person's *casta* in baptismal or census records. In the last decades of the Vice-Royalty, the ostensibly racial classification had become quite flexible and bore only an approximate relationship to genetic reality. Certain racial fictions, such as that of the "whiteness" of the creoles, even became accepted in the etiquette of good manners.

Third, the continuing and parallel processes of hispanization and mestizoization contributed to a blurring of both ethnic and racial distinctions and to an ever-decreasing overlap between racial and cultural lines of cleavage in Mexican society. Paradoxically, the very brutality with which the Spaniards annihilated indigenous civilizations, the arrogance with which they imposed their religion, language, and customs, the ruthlessness with which they reduced Indians to the status of helpless *peones*, the callousness with which they exerted their *droit de cuissage* over the conquered women, all contributed to the cultural and genetic homogenization of the population. In short, the shattering ruthlessness of Spanish colonialism, particularly in its early phases, led in the long run to the relatively harmonious syncretism of modern Mexico.

Fourth, the Catholic Church was, of course, part and parcel of the colonial regime. As the empire's largest landowner, it was by the same token the greatest exploiter of *peones* in Mexico. Through the Inquisition, it exercised its tyranny over the minds and bodies of men. As late as the 1810s, the Inquisition's only concession to the changing times was that it executed heretics by a firing squad instead of burning them at the stake. Nevertheless, in spite of this damning indictment, the Church did play a humanizing and universalistic role in the area of race. Church prelates put a stop to the enslavement of Indians and mitigated that of Africans. The Church refused to accept the validity of racial distinctions. Behind every face, no matter how swarthy, it found a soul to save, by force if necessary.

Finally, the very concern for physical appearance and its consequent elaborate taxonomy of racial phenotypes militated against the drawing of rigid color lines. The minutia with which shades of color were distinguished and the complexity of a terminology which reserved a special term for every possible crossing of Indian, European, and African over at least three generations greatly lowered the reliability and validity of classification. By the time of Independence the social validity of these terms was practically nil, and racial labeling was little more than a narcissistic salon game for bored aristocrats and erudite pedants. The system broke down under the weight of its own complexity and thus favored rather than hindered racial mobility. Mexico had indeed become a nation of bronze.

NOTES

[1] See his *La Población Negra de Mexico* and *El Proceso de Aculturación.* This chapter owes much to both these books which have been undeservedly neglected by North American and European scholars. Aguirre Beltrán's work represents dynamic anthropology and social history at their best and constitutes a much more adequate model for Meso-American scholarship than, for example, the more widely known and quoted work of Redfield.

[2] Bernal Diaz del Castillo, *The True History of the Conquest of New Spain.*

[3] Gonzalo Aguirre Beltrán, *La Población Negra de Mexico,* pp. 213, 221; *El Proceso de Aculturación,* pp. 31, 68.

[4] Aguirre Beltrán, *La Población,* p. 237; Carlos Basauri, *La Población Indígena de México,* pp. 113, 125. Charles Wagley and Marvin Harris, *Minorities in the New World,* p. 82.

[5] Altogether some 40 Indian languages are spoken in Mexico, some of the principal ones being Nahuatl, Zapotec, Tzotzil, Tzeltal, Otomi, Mixtec, Chol, Totonac, Chinantec, Mazatec and Maya. The Indian minorities are quite unevenly distributed in Mexico to the extent of constituting majorities in certain local areas such as the Chiapas highlands. In 1960 90.6 per cent of the Mexican Indians were concentrated in ten of the thirty-two states in the Republic; 22.6 per cent lived in Oaxaca, 12.6 per cent in Chiapas, 10.3 per cent in Veracruz, 9.8 per cent in Yucatán, 9.7 per cent in Puebla, 7.7 per cent in Hidalgo, 6.6 per cent in Guerrero, 5.6 per cent in Mexico, 3.8 per cent in San Luis Potosí, and 1.9 per cent in Michoacán.

[6] *Source:* Aguirre Beltrán, *La Población,* p. 237. The last two columns of the table became increasingly lumped together into a single mestizo group.

[7] See Benjamin N. Colby and Pierre L. van den Berghe, "Ethnic Relations in Southeastern Mexico"; and Pierre L. van den Berghe and Benjamin N. Colby, "Ladino-Indian Relations in the Highlands of Chiapas, Mexico." For a somewhat similar situation in neighboring Guatemala, see Melvin Tumin, *Caste in a Peasant Society.* See also Julio de la Fuente, *Relacions Interétnicas,* Chapters 11 and 12.

III

Brazil

Ethnic and race relations in Brazil exceed in complexity the Mexican situation. This is hardly surprising, for Brazil is more a subcontinent than a country, and dwarfs in both population and area all other Latin American nations. Regional differences and cultural pluralism are probably more salient in Brazil than in any other society of the Western Hemisphere with the exception of Canada.

Thanks to the works of Brazilians like Gilberto Freyre and Florestan Fernandes, North Americans like Charles Wagley, Marvin Harris, and Donald Pierson, and Europeans like Roger Bastide, ethnic and race relations are better documented in Brazil than in Mexico, although not nearly as well as in the United States [1]. The most distinguished scholar in this field is Gilberto Freyre, whose works have not only documented Brazilian slave society, but have also been influential in creating the partly undeserved reputation of Brazil as a "racial paradise." Freyre certainly does not idealize Brazilian slavery; in fact, he describes in highly critical terms the decadent, sadistic, indolent, syphilis-ridden, slave-owning aristocracy of northeastern Brazil in the eighteenth and nineteenth centuries; however, he does tend to minimize the amount of racial conflict in contemporary Brazil by ascribing tensions to class factors. Donald Pierson and other

North American scholars have adopted the same viewpoint, and, by comparison with the situation in the United States, they are certainly correct in stressing the flexibility of racial distinctions in Brazil [2]. Other studies, however, have shown that considerable racial prejudice exists in Brazil and that racial discrimination does not disappear if one controls for class [3].

When Pedro Alvares Cabral sighted Brazil in 1500, Portugal claimed it as hers, but it was not until 1532 that an effective colonial government was established and that regular contact between the two countries was initiated. Although the French and the Dutch contested Portuguese control over Brazil in the sixteenth and seventeenth centuries and at times occupied parts of it, the country remained a Portuguese colony until 1822 and continued to be linked to Portugal through dynastic and cultural ties during the Brazilian Empire (1822–1889). The Portuguese encountered along the northern coast of Brazil a number of small, sparsely settled, nomadic, Tupi-speaking Indian groups which lacked large-scale centralized states and could offer no serious resistance to the Europeans. For a short period peaceful trade was established between the Indians and Portuguese, but the greed of the Portuguese for gold, diamonds, and slaves soon made them turn to violence [4]. By the mid-sixteenth century, they had begun to organize slave-hunting expeditions (*bandeiras*) into the interior, often led by mestizos known as *bandeirantes, paulistas,* or *mamelucos.* Like most nomads the Indians made poor slaves, and epidemic diseases such as smallpox, measles, and the common cold decimated an already sparse population that lacked any immunity against these imported plagues. In the absence of Portuguese women there was considerable miscegenation between Indian women and Portuguese men from the very beginning [5]. A climate of promiscuous hedonism pervaded Brazilian society, and a French visitor speaking of Brazilians said: "Ils aiment le sexe à la folie" [6].

Because of the scarcity and unreliability of Indian slaves, the Portuguese quickly turned to Africa as the main source of servile labor. The first Negro slave entered Brazil in 1538, and a slave market was established at Salvador de Bahia. As the *bandeirantes* continued to raid the interior for Indian slaves, they encountered increasing opposition from the Jesuits who were trying to convert and control the aboriginal population by concentrating it in mission villages *(aldeas)*. The *paulistas* often attacked these *aldeas* in their quest for slaves until in 1574 a royal decree prohibited raids on the Jesuit missions. This futher stimulated the African slave trade, which steadily increased in scope throughout the sixteenth and seventeenth centuries and indeed up to its abolition in the mid-nineteenth century.

Brazil's massive reliance on the African slave trade is one of the central facts of its history. The forced immigration of Negroes coming mostly from West Africa, Angola, and Mozambique lasted over three centuries. Although Brazil under British pressure agreed to abolish the trade in 1831, contraband slaves continued to be imported until 1853. During the slaving period between three and five million Africans entered Brazil and settled mostly in the northeastern provinces of Bahia, Maranhão, and Pernambuco and to a lesser extent in Rio. Slaving was most intense during the last century of the traffic. In 1781, 50 vessels were engaged in the trade, and in 1848 alone some 60,000 Africans entered the country [7]. West Africans, many of whom were Muslims, predominated in Bahia, but in Pernambuco and in the south Bantu-speaking peoples from Central and Eastern Africa were found in great number.

Unlike in the United States where slavery nearly obliterated all traces of African culture, the African contribution to the national culture of Brazil was appreciable. This is clearly evident in religious and magical rites and beliefs (practiced, for example, in the *candomblé*), in the *cuisine*, in the folk tales, and in the vocabulary and syntax of American Portuguese.

The demographic impact of Africans on the Brazilian population was very great from the eighteenth century to the closing decades of the nineteenth century. With the massive importation of Negroes, whites and near-whites were rapidly outnumbered in Brazil as a whole, and particularly in the northeastern districts. In 1789, out of a total population of 2.3 million, 1.5 million were African slaves, a figure which probably included the mulattoes. In 1835 only 24.4 per cent of the total Brazilian population were classified as white. By 1872 out of a total of 9.9 million, the white percentage had climbed to 38.1 per cent, partly as a result of the end of the slave trade and the beginning of large-scale immigration from Europe, and partly, no doubt, because of a more elastic definition of "white." Slaves had declined to 15.2 per cent of the total, for manumission was becoming increasingly frequent; American Indians numbered slightly under 4 per cent; the remaining 42.7 per cent consisted of free people of color, mostly mulattoes and mestizos [8].

Through large-scale immigration from Europe "whites" came to outnumber Negroes and mulattoes in the twentieth century. This process is referred to in Brazil as "bleaching." However, intensive miscegenation and the lack of a clear-cut social definition of race make an even approximate estimate of the "racial" composition of Brazil hazardous. A 1941 estimate breaks down the population as follows: 2.2 per cent Indian, 15.5 per cent mestizo, 37.2 per cent Negroes and mulattoes, 44.4 per cent white, and 0.7 per cent Asian [9]. De Azevedo, however, quotes the following figures for 1935: 60 per cent white, 32 per cent mestizo and mulatto, and 8 per cent Negro [10]. Through extensive "passing," the white percentage bears little relationship to any genetic classification; rather it reflects a comprehensive social category that includes nearly all people whose ancestry is predominantly European.

Colonial and Imperial Brazil can be divided conveniently into two major zones from the point of view of race relations. The coastal regions were inhabited principally by Negroes, mulattoes, and whites. The areas of greatest African concentration were the northeastern provinces (capitanias) of Bahia, Maranhão, and Pernambuco. This region was also the cultural and economic center of gravity of Brazil until the mid-nineteenth century; the cities of Salvador and Recife competed with Rio and completely eclipsed São Paulo as centers of Brazilian culture. On the other hand, the provinces of the interior (sertão) were settled mostly by small groups of adventurers and slave-hunters (bandeirantes, paulistas) and inhabited by Indians and westernized mestizos generically referred to as caboclos. This does not imply that there were no Negroes in the interior and no mestizos along the coast. For example, when gold and later diamond deposits were discovered in the present state of Minas Gerais in the late seventeenth and early eighteenth centuries, numerous Negro slaves were brought in to work on the mines. In addition, fugitive slaves sought refuge in the backlands, where they established settlements (*quilombos*) and intermixed with Indian women.

However, the regional concentration of Negroes in the northeast broke down on a large scale only with the economic development of the south. The expansion of coffee production which started in the mid-nineteenth century was followed by industrialization and the rise of São Paulo and Rio de Janeiro as the two great metropolises of Brazil. This great shift in the country's economic center of gravity from the north to the south was, of course, accompanied by considerable Negro migration to the southern metropolises, and hence by a greater dispersion of the Afro-Brazilian population. The rubber boom in the Amazon basin during the last decades of the nineteenth century until 1912 also brought about a greater racial mixture as Negroes and whites entered a hitherto overwhelmingly Indian and mestizo part of Brazil. However, by the time of World War I the rubber bubble had burst and the large Amazon boom towns of Manaus and Belém were in full decline.

Let us return to the two major zones of interracial contact— the interior and the coastal area during the Colonial and Imperial periods. In each zone a pattern of race and ethnic relations developed which was crucial to the development of the national culture of Brazil and which conformed in every major respect to our paternalistic model. In the interior the Jesuits established their theocratic brand of paternalism by settling the Indians on their *aldeas*. The Jesuits regarded the Indians as their wards and cast themselves in the role of spiritual mentors and protectors of the Indians against the depredations of the *paulistas* and *bandeirantes*. This long-standing conflict of interests between the Society of Jesus and the lay Portuguese settlers finally came to a head when the Marquis of Pombal (King José I's Prime Minister) expelled the Jesuits from Brazil in 1758.

The mission village or *aldea* was, like the slave plantation, an economically, religiously, and politically autonomous microcosm. In fact, the Jesuits deliberately created a new culture and society according to their vision of what was good for the Indians. Under their authoritarian and patriarchal guidance they forcibly separated children from their parents, they reshaped Indian societies according to their own utopia, and they modified, fused, and standardized Tupi languages, thereby creating *lingua geral* ("general language"), which became the most widely spoken instrument of communication between the *caboclos* of the interior. It was through the medium of *lingua geral* that Indians were converted to Catholicism, often by force [11], and it might be said that the Jesuits imposed on the Indians an artificially created "Jesuit culture," rather than Portuguese culture. If the Jesuits hindered the physical extermination of the Indians by the *bandeirantes*, they contributed powerfully to the disintegration of Indian cultures by prohibiting polygyny and preferential cross-cousin marriage which were basic features of the social organization of most Indian groups in the area. The *aldea* was the Jesuits' vision of the City of God on earth.

Through the *aldeas* the Society of Jesus created a new population and a new society in the interior of Brazil. The *caboclos* are in large measure the mestizoized, Christianized, partly westernized descendants of the Indians who were colonized by the Jesuits and who now constitute the mass of the semi-subsistence peasantry. In Brazil the countervailing interests and influence of the lay settlers limited and eventually broke down the political power of the Jesuits as a benevolently despotic upper caste ruling over the Indians and mestizos of the interior, but in the more remote Paraguay the Society managed to constitute a virtually autonomous theocracy within the Spanish Empire.

In contrast to the stern, other-worldly, and theocratic brand of paternalism prevailing in the Jesuit missions, a sensual, lay, aristocratic form of paternalism developed in the sugar-cane plantations (*fazendas*) of Pernambuco and Bahia. This model of feudal patriarchalism made at least as strong an impact in determining Brazilian national culture as did the Jesuit *aldeas*. The *fazendas* had their economic basis in slavery and in what Freyre aptly called "latifundiary monoculture," that is, the cultivation of a single dominant cash crop on large estates owned by a feudal gentry. (A small peasantry of mestizos and mulattoes existed side by side with the owners of *latifundios* of the northeast, however.) Gradually, African slavery supplanted the enslavement of Indians which was finally outlawed in 1611. The classical analysis of this system in Freyre's *The Masters and the Slaves* depicts the Portuguese planters as a slothful, sadistic, decadent, vicious, syphilitic, sensuous aristocracy linked in an ambivalently affectionate symbiosis with a masochistic class of Negro slaves whom they dragged through forced miscegenation in the indolent cesspool of their refined perversions. In Freyre's vivid words:

> "Slothful but filled to overflowing with sexual concerns, the life of the sugarplanter tended to become a life that was lived in a hammock. A stationary hammock, with the master taking his ease, sleeping, dozing. Or a hammock on the move, with the master on a journey or a promenade beneath the heavy draperies or curtains. Or again, a squeaking hammock, with the master copulating in it" [12].

No doubt Freyre's strongly psychoanalytical orientation and his focus on the sexual aspect of race relations give a somewhat unbalanced picture of Brazilian slavery. Nevertheless it is clear that the *fazenda* was a classic example of paternalistic race relations. It was a self-sufficient microcosm with its own food supply, repair shops, chapel, resident priest-tutor, cemetery, hospital, and school. Politically, the *fazenda* enjoyed much *de facto* autonomy and provided for its own defense, often being fortified against attacks by the Dutch, the French, and other European interlopers along the northeastern coast. The typical *fazenda* was larger than the average southern United States plantation. Eighty slaves seem to have been a minimum for a profitable sugar estate, and a number of them probably had as many as 200 Negroes. Many plantations had their own little animal- or water-driven cane-crushing mill. (The word *engenho,* meaning "mill" or "engine," was often used as a synonym for a sugar plantation.)

Residentially, the big house (*casa grande*), inhabited by the owner's family and by domestic slaves, dominated the nearby slave quarters (*senzala*) that housed the field hands and skilled craftsmen. Relations between masters and house slaves were intimate, that is, both spatially and emotionally close, though socially very distant. White children were raised by Negro wet-nurses (*amas*) and given a slave of their age and sex as play companions. When a white boy reached sexual maturity, he was sexually initiated with one of his father's slaves and continued to engage in promiscuous concubinage with female slaves throughout his sexually active lifetime. Interracial concubinage with female slaves was completely accepted for white men, and, according to the dual standard of sexual morality, marriage was not considered an impediment to the maintenance of a slave harem. Even the Catholic clergy interbred extensively with women of color. The *morena* (a straight-haired woman of medium-brown skin color) rather than the white woman has traditionally been considered the ideal of feminine beauty in Brazil, and some intermarriage between light-skinned mulatto women and Portuguese men did take place.

The division of labor along racial lines was quite clear-cut. The Portuguese aristocracy was a leisure class *par excellence,* engaged almost solely in war and love making. All the productive work in agriculture and handicraft was a monopoly of the slaves. Among the slaves the house servants (concubines, maids, cooks, wet nurses, and butlers) constituted an elite that lived in the big house in close contact with their masters whom they came increasingly to resemble culturally as well as physically through miscegenation. Such lusitanized slaves were referred to as *ladinos* to distinguish them from the nonwesternized slaves fresh from Africa. Young Negroes brought up in the big house were known as *crias.*

Social distance between masters and slaves was maintained through a punctilious etiquette of subservience and dominance. Sumptuary regulations, forms of address, and symbolic gestures regulated social intercourse between people of vastly different status who were in constant and intimate contact with each other. For example, masters were carried about in litters and were accompanied by a retinue of slaves arranged in a well-regulated procession when going to public places. Negroes were forbidden to wear gold jewels and weapons [13]. On the *fazendas* the master of the estate and his family led the slaves in a highly ritualized form of common worship. Status distinctions were manifest in all types of interaction.

Many stereotypes about the Negro developed during the slavery period and are still part of the Brazilian folklore. The Afro-Brazilian was regarded as a lascivious, physically unattractive, happy-go-lucky, grownup child. In the words of a modern Brazilian author who accepts these stereotypes, "the Negro element in general revealed a perpetual good humor, a childish and expansive joy, a delight in the lightest incidents of life. Nothing gave him greater happiness than to dance, to sing, to clothe himself elaborately and in gaudy colors. Filled with the joy of youth, a ray of sunshine illuminated his childish soul" [14].

Because of the mitigating influence of the Catholic Church which insisted on the baptism of slaves, favored manumission, encouraged marriage of slaves, and sought to limit the arbitrary power of slave-owners, Brazilian slavery was less brutal than that prevailing in the southern United States. Although Brazil was the last major nation in the Western cultural orbit finally to abolish slavery (it did so without compensation to owners in 1888), considerable emancipation had taken place before. Favorite servants, concubines, and illegitimate children were frequently manumitted either during the lifetime of their masters or by testament. Slaves could accumulate property and buy their freedom. In 1871 the Brazilian parliament passed a law emancipating all children born of slave mothers after that date.

In theory the only legal distinction was between slave and freeman, but in fact free Negroes and mulattoes were discriminated against unless they were light enough to "pass" for white. Free Afro-Brazilians remained confined largely to manual occupations (as they still are today to a considerable degree), and they were *de facto* excluded from the priesthood and from higher government positions. There was also racial segregation in the colonial army. Manual labor became intimately linked with color, as testified to by the Brazilian proverb: "Work is for Negroes and dogs" [15].

Of course, slavery was no more idyllic in Brazil than elsewhere. There is considerable evidence that some slaves adjusted to their condition; this seems to have been particularly true of the *ladino* house slaves born and raised in slavery. However, many newly imported slaves regained their freedom by seeking refuge in the "runaway" settlements (*quilombos*) of the interior. In addition, slave revolts, often led by free Negroes or by literate Muslims from the Sudan, were fairly common and were brutally crushed. Alone in the Bahia province in the early nineteenth century there were uprisings in 1807, 1809, 1813, 1826, 1827, 1830, and 1835. The last uprising almost took on the character of a Muslim

Holy War, but all these insurrections failed because many slaves refused to take part in them and warned their masters of the plots [16].

During the second half of the nineteenth century, the northeast was beginning to lose its economic and cultural paramountcy in Brazil. The decline of sugar was accompanied by the temporary rubber boom in the Amazon basin where slavery had gained virtually no foothold, and by the more permanent expansion of coffee production of the São Paulo region where European immigrants gradually supplanted Negroes as an agricultural labor force. Between 1820 and 1930 approximately 4,000,000 white immigrants entered Brazil, mostly Portuguese, Italians, Spaniards, and Germans. They created a large white working class that competed with Negro labor, and hence undermined the economic basis of slavery.

These economic and demographic factors, combined with a vigorous abolitionist movement in which Joaquim Nabuco was the most prominent figure, led to the gradual and peaceful demise of Brazil's "peculiar institution" (to borrow a common euphemism of the ante-bellum southern United States). Nevertheless the feudal slave-owning aristocracy was still powerful enough to help the army topple the monarchy when the Emperor sided with the abolitionists. The Empire survived slavery by a bare eighteen months, and was overthrown by a bloodless military coup on November 14, 1889. This dual transformation ushered Brazil into its modern period.

Notwithstanding the pervasive influence of slavery on the Brazilian social structure, Brazil never developed a system of racial estates like the *castas* of colonial Mexico. As with the Spaniards in Mexico, Portuguese colonization was accompanied by a dual process of miscegenation and westernization involving the European, African, and indigenous population. However, the Brazilian colonial structure was politically less centralized. The slave-owning aristocracy of the northeast, the Jesuit missions, the *paulistas,* and the settlers of the *sertão* all retained considerable local autonomy in a land of which much still remains a vast moving frontier. Through a succession of economic booms and depressions (involving the production of sugar, gold, diamonds, rubber, and coffee) vast movements of population altered both the racial composition and distribution of Brazilians in a way which made at once for regional differentiation and national homogenization. This fluid and decentralized situation defeated any attempt to classify the population into well-defined racial categories valid throughout Brazil. Yet, and this is one of the paradoxes of Brazilian society, this fact does not mean that Brazil is free of racial consciousness, prejudice, and discrimination. As we shall see presently, the salience of race is much greater in Brazil than in Mexico, although much lesser than in the United States or South Africa.

What, then, is modern Brazil like in terms of race and ethnic relations? The official ideology, of which Gilberto Freyre has become the most erudite and distinguished spokesman, claims that there is virtually no racial problem in Brazil. The rather high correlation between socioeconomic status and physical appearance (e.g., the poverty and menial occupations of most Afro-Brazilians) is explained in terms of the heritage of slavery rather than in terms of current racial discrimination. As for *prima facie* evidence of racial discrimination and prejudice, it is dismissed as representing *class* factors. Control for class, says the "official line," and what appears to be racial discrimination or prejudice will vanish completely or nearly so.

In a land in which race and class are so closely correlated this position has some plausibility and can even muster some evidence. For example, the saying that "money bleaches" suggests that the achievement of high socioeconomic status can overcome the stigma of race and transform one into a "social white." Similarly, "passing" into the "white" group has been much easier in Brazil than in the United States or South Africa. But even if nothing more was attached to an obviously African or Indian ancestry than the presumption of low class status, it would still be a serious handicap and a distinctly racial one. Actually, many facts of the racial situation in contemporary Brazil make the "official view" untenable.

Before I present the evidence to support my contention that an *appreciable amount of distinctly racial prejudice and discrimination exists in modern Brazil,* I must also stress that racism has always been officially condemned by both church and state, and that neither has practiced it in recent times. Furthermore, the Indian policy of the government initiated in 1910 by the *Serviço de Proteçao aos Indios* under the leadership of Candido Mariano da Silva Rondon has been exemplary in its selflessness, humanitarianism, respect for indigenous cultures, and methods of noncoercive assimilation. The distance, however, from the lofty ideals to the actual practice is great.

The post-World War II studies sponsored by UNESCO in various parts of Brazil, the work of Wagley in the Amazon basin, the investigations of Bastide and Fernandes in the São Paulo area, as well as other more limited studies, all point to the existence of considerable racism in various parts of modern Brazil [17]. Although great regional variations in the specific morphology of racial prejudice and discrimination and in the social hierarchy of racial groups make generalizations about Brazil as a whole difficult, I would claim that *during the twentieth century Brazil has moved away from its old paternalistic type of race relations toward the competitive model.*

To be sure, the intensity of racial conflict is much lower in Brazil than in the United States or South Africa, but nevertheless a racial syndrome exists that simply cannot be dismissed as a class prejudice. This seems to be especially true in the large urban centers of southern Brazil (Rio and São Paulo). The northeast and the Amazon basin have to some extent escaped the economic and demographic transformations of the south, and have changed less rapidly. In the south, however, and in some degree elsewhere, the dynamics of industrialization, of rapid urbanization (São Paulo grew from 44,000 in 1886 to 240,000 in 1900, to 2,200,000 in 1950), and of massive European immigration have profoundly transformed race relations.

Competition in unskilled and semi-skilled occupations between Negroes and white immigrants replaced the old master and servant relationship. Impersonal, segmentary contacts in large cities were substituted for the close, face-to-face, diffuse ties in the agrarian microcosm of the plantation. Mechanisms of social distance such as etiquette broke down, to be replaced in many cases by spatial segregation. Miscegenation became less common as the exploitative form of patriarchal concubinage became obsolete and as contacts across racial lines decreased in frequency. As for the remaining Indian minorities, they continued to be exploited by the frontier settlers and decimated by epidemic diseases without being effectively integrated into the national culture [18].

More specifically, what evidence is there for the existence of a "competitive" type of racial prejudice and discrimination in modern Brazil?

1. Even though there have never been any clear-cut racial lines separating one group from another, Brazilians are very concious of physical appearance and have developed an elaborate nomenclature to designate varying combinations of skin color, facial features (such as shape of nose and lips), and hair texture (straight, curly, or kinky). Among the racial terms used are *branco, branco de Bahia, cabra, cobo verde, mameluco, caboré, cafuso, mazombo, mucama, muleque, mulecote, moreno, mina, pardavasco, preto, pardo, caboclo, mulato, preto retinto, escuro,* and some others. Few if any of these words describe well-defined groups, and the images evoked by each would vary from region to region; even the vocabulary of racial typology changes from one part of the country to another. Furthermore, such fine distinctions of phenotype are drawn that siblings would often be classified differently by the same person, or different judges would disagree over the correct racial label to be given to the same person. *This very consciousness of, and concern for, physical appearance has thus paradoxically militated against the drawing of precise color lines between distinct groups.*

It might be argued that these racial labels are purely descriptive, hence that they do not constitute evidence of racial prejudice. This, however, is not the case, for in Brazilian culture distinct esthetic canons lead one to regard certain types as more attractive than others. For example, light brown skin is valued over both pale and dark skin; straight hair is considered "better" than curly or kinky hair; and facial features approximating the Negroid type are generally regarded as ugly. Derogatory sayings stressing the unattractiveness of Negroes are found in the Brazilian folklore (e.g., "the Negro has an ugly face" or "the Negro has no face—he has a tin can") [19].

2. In addition to this racial nomenclature, and the esthetic value-judgments connected with it, racial stereotypes concerning

the alleged moral, intellectual, and social qualities of members of certain groups are widely held in Brazil. Thus in the Amazon the *caboclo* is regarded as lazy, tricky, suspicious, and timid [20]. Most deprecating are the stereotypes against Afro-Brazilians. The Brazilian folklore abounds with such proverbs and sayings as: "The Negro doesn't sit down, he squats"; "The Negro's intelligence is the same size as his hair"; "The Negro doesn't marry, he gets together"; "An old nigger when he dies stinks like hell"; and "The Negro is an ass and a brute" [21]. In a study taken among teachers' college students in São Paulo not a single one of the 580 subjects rejected all anti-Negro stereotypes from a checklist of 41 items. Seventy-five per cent of the sample accepted 23 or more stereotypes [22]. In the old plantation region of Bahia the paternalistic stereotypes of the Negroes as humble, loyal, servile, affectionate to their employers, cheerful, and content with their humble fate are still surviving [23]. In the cities of the south, however, the whites deplore the disappearance of the "old Negroes" and consider the new generation of Negroes as arrogant, aggressive, immoral, sexually perverse, physically unattractive, and superstitious [24]. Pungent body order, sexual potency, sense of humor, physical strength, and musical ability are also traits commonly attributed to Negroes. Mulattoes, who have been socially more mobile than Negroes, are held to be pretentious, arrogant, unreliable, boastful, "cheeky," jealous of the whites, and social climbers [25].

3. Although the boundaries of racial groups are not clearly defined and although there exists some regional variation in the hierarchy, the three parent stocks of the Brazilian population are ranked in terms of status, with the European stock on top, the African at the bottom, and the indigenous in the intermediate position. Wagley reports that in his Amazon town Negroes rank higher than Indians or *caboclos* [26], but in the country at large the reverse is true. Admittedly, group lines can be crossed with some ease, and social mobility can overcome to some extent low racial status. A Brazilian expression goes: "A rich Negro is a white and a poor white is a Negro." Nevertheless race is not only empirically correlated with class; it remains a significant determinant of status after class has been controlled for. Again the

folklore reflects this racial hierarchy. A Brazilian song goes as follows:

> The white man eats in the parlor,
> The Indian in the hall,
> The mulatto in the kitchen,
> The Negro in the privy.

4. Miscegenation in Brazil is probably becoming less and less common between persons of widely different color. Interracial concubinage, although still existing and not seriously disapproved of, is less and less common [27]. Intermarriage between persons of widely different physical appearance is both rare and subject to social disapproval. Of a total of 1269 marriages in Bahia in 1933-1934 only 42 were between persons classified by Pierson as belonging to different racial groups [28]. In Bahia, 93 per cent of a sample of white students objected to marrying a Negro; in São Paulo 95 per cent of the white students said that they would not marry a Negro and 87 per cent that they would not marry a light-skinned mulatto [29].

5. Segregation and discrimination though never legalized are frequently present in some form in Brazil. Pierson has argued that segregation is more along class lines than along racial lines [30]. However, it seems that, all other criteria of status being equal, nonwhite racial characteristics are a serious and probably increasing handicap [31]. Although 92 per cent of the students in the São Paulo study were willing to grant Negroes a theoretical equality of rights and opportunities in accordance with the Brazilian ethos, only 60 per cent accepted casual relations between Negroes and whites, and only 38 per cent tolerated close emotional or amicable relationships with Negroes [32].

In a study of residential segregation in the state of São Paulo it was found that colored persons lived in a separate section in 19 out of the 36 towns studied, although that situation was, at least in part, a function of socioeconomic factors [33]. Similarly, Pierson reports extensive residential segregation along racial lines in the city of São Paulo [34]. Customary segregation is reported in public parks, barber shops, private clubs and associations, in some cinemas and at sport events because of price differences in entrance tickets, and in public or semi-public dances and at parties [35]. In a study of 245 newspaper advertisements for domestic servants, *all* prospective employers requested white servants [36]. Lest we should distort the picture, none of these practices is general throughout Brazil nor are they rigidly enforced. In fact, most Brazilians probably disapprove of them, at least in theory.

This evidence suggests that Brazil has been moving toward a competitive type of prejudice and race relations. For a number of historical and sociological reasons suggested earlier (role of the Catholic Church, peaceful abolition of slavery, blurring of color lines), the intensity of racial prejudice in Brazil has been relatively low. The northern states showed until recently many paternalistic survivals, such as tolerance of concubinage, elaborate racial etiquette, and close face-to-face relationships between the white aristocrats and plantation labor [37]. On the other hand, the most competitive form of race relations is found in the south, particularly in São Paulo. This is to be expected, for this region has become industrialized very fast and has many lower-class white immigrants in economic competition with Negroes [38].

Several observers and students of Brazilian race relations have noted that racial consciousness, prejudice, and discrimination are on the increase in the southern part of the country [39]. Marvin Harris, in a detailed field study of a small town in central Brazil, also reports a definite shift toward more and more competitive relations. The socioeconomic gap between whites and nonwhites is not very wide there, and both groups compete for manual jobs. Race relations are considerably tenser than in three other communities studied at the same time. The town is split into two classes, the whites (or *brancos*) and the Negroes (or *pretos*), which are rapidly becoming racial castes. The Negroes have developed their parallel institutions, clubs, religious festivals, music bands, and carnivals. Segregation and discrimination are increasingly rigid [40].

Rising anti-Negro prejudice in São Paulo, Rio de Janeiro, and elsewhere caused the National Congress to pass a law after World War II making racial discrimination a criminal offense [41]. Such a law had never been necessary before. Even in the cradle of paternalism around Bahia agriculture is being mechanized, and the old emotional ties between white landowners and Negro workers are breaking down. Large industrial sugar mills have replaced the small plantation mills, and the field hands no longer have personal ties to the white employers [42].

In an attempt to refute the "official view" that "Brazil has no racial problem" I may have overstated the case. All things considered Brazil is probably nearer the pole of tolerance approximated in Mexico than the pole of extreme bigotry represented by South Africa. Furthermore, present trends may be reversed, and Brazil may yet evolve from a relatively mild form of competitive race relations to a genuinely egalitarian society as far as race is concerned. At present, however, Brazil may be more aptly described as a racial purgatory than as a racial paradise.

NOTES

[1] See bibliography, in particular, Gilberto Freyre's *The Masters and the Slaves* and *The Mansions and the Shanties.*

[2] Cf. Donald Pierson, *Negroes in Brazil.*

[3] Cf. Charles Wagley, *Race and Class in Rural Brazil;* Roger Bastide and Pierre van den Berghe, "Stereotoypes, Norms and Interracial Behavior in São Paulo"; and Roger Bastide and Florestan Fernandes, *Brancos e Negros em São Paulo.*

[4] This deterioration in early Portuguese-Indian contacts during the first half of the fifteenth century has been studied by Alexander Marchant in his book *From Barter to Slavery.*

[5] In Gilberto Freyre's vivid prose "No sooner had the European leaped ashore than he found his feet slipping among the naked Indian women, and the very fathers of the Society of Jesus had to take care not to sink into the carnal mire." Cf. *The Masters and the Slaves,* p. 83.

[6] Quoted in Gilberto Freyre, *op. cit.,* p. 389; see also *ibid.,* pp. 348–353.

[7] Evaristo de Moraes, *A Escravidão Africana no Brasil,* p. 82.

[8] Fernando de Azevedo, *Brazilian Culture,* pp. 31, 34, 38.

[9] *Encyclopedia Britannica,* 1960, p. 55.

[10] De Azevedo, *op. cit.,* p. 38.

[11] In the words of José de Anchieta, a pious and saintly father of the Society, "the sword and the iron rod are the best kind of preaching." Quoted by Freyre, *op. cit.,* p. 141.

[12] Freyre, *op. cit.,* p. 380.

[13] Donald Pierson, *Negroes in Brazil,* pp. 76–78, 81–82; Freyre, *The Mansions and the Shanties,* pp. 81, 261.

[14] João Pandiá Calogeras, *A History of Brazil*, p. 29.

[15] Pierson, *op. cit.*, p. 69.

[16] *Ibid.*, pp. 7, 40–41, 44.

[17] Charles Wagley, ed., *Race and Class in Rural Brazil;* Charles Wagley, *Amazon Town;* Thales de Azevedo, *Les Elites de Couleur dans une Ville Brésilienne;* Roger Bastide and Florestan Fernandes, *Brancos e Negros em São Paulo;* Roger Bastide and Pierre van den Berghe, "Stereotypes, Norms and Interracial Behavior in São Paulo, Brazil"; and Emilio Willems, "Racial Attitudes in Brazil."

[18] Charles Wagley and Marvin Harris, *Minorities in the New World,* pp. 44–46.

[19] Charles Wagley, ed., *Race and Class in Rural Brazil,* pp. 35, 55–56.

[20] Charles Wagley, *Amazon Town,* p. 141.

[21] Charles Wagley, ed., *Race and Class in Rural Brazil,* pp. 35, 55–56; Gilberto Freyre, *The Mansions and the Shanties,* p. 409.

[22] Cf. Bastide and van den Berghe, *op. cit.*, p. 691.

[23] Wagley, *op. cit.*, pp. 32–34.

[24] Bastide and van den Berghe, *op. cit.*, p. 691; Andrew W. Lind, ed., *Race Relations in World Perspective,* pp. 452–458.

[25] Wagley, *op. cit.*, pp. 32–34.

[26] Wagley, *Amazon Town,* p. 141.

[27] Pierson, *op. cit.*, p. 123; Wagley, ed., *Race and Class in Rural Brazil,* pp. 39–41.

[28] Pierson, *op. cit.*, p. 147.

[29] Bastide and van den Berghe, *op. cit.*, p. 692; Pierson, *op. cit.*, p. 148.

[30] *Ibid.*, pp. 178–218, 348–349.

[31] Wagley, *op. cit.*, pp. 80–81, 88–89, 155.

[32] Bastide and van den Berghe, *op. cit.*, p. 692.

[33] Emilio Willems, *op. cit.*, p. 402.

[34] Andrew W. Lind, *op. cit.*, pp. 452–458.

[35] Pierson, *op. cit.*, pp. 184–187, 195–196, 198, 202–203; Lind, *op. cit.*, pp. 452–458; Wagley, *op. cit.*, p. 72; Willems, *op. cit.*, p. 402.

[36] Willems, *op. cit.*, p. 402.

[37] Pierson, *op. cit.*, pp. 226, 327–329; Wagley, *op. cit.*, pp. 22, 23–27, 32–34.

[38] Lind, *op. cit.*, p. 461. These southern findings do not, however, seem to be entirely nor even predominantly attributable to the racial prejudices of recent European immigrants, as suggested by those who claim that racism is alien to Portuguese and Brazilian culture. The Bastide and van den Berghe study showed no clear-cut differences between first-generation and older-stock Brazilians. Cf. *op. cit.*, p. 693.

[39] Pierson, *op. cit.*, p. 342; Lind, *op. cit.*, pp. 459, 461; Wagley, *op. cit.*, p. 155.

[40] Wagley, *op. cit.*, pp. 72–81.

[41] Wagley, *op. cit.*, p. 8.

[42] Wagley, *op. cit.*, pp. 21–22.

IV

The United States

Historiography might be defined as a new secularized way of creating a country's national mythology. This chapter takes issue with a long tradition of ethnocentrism and racism in the study of United States history. My central thesis is that, with the early development and later florescence of racism in the United States, this republic has been, since its birth and until World War II, a *"Herrenvolk* democracy" [1].

The American "Revolution" was in fact a movement of political emancipation by a section of the white settlers against control from England. That many of its leaders had been exposed to the French Enlightenment and used the rhetoric of freedom has led to the "official" interpretation of the American Revolution as a democratic, equalitarian, and libertarian movement similar to that of the French Revolution. Although a few idealists like John Quincy Adams interpreted the Declaration of Independence literally to apply to all people, and though a few more like Jefferson were perturbed by the contradiction between the libertarian rhetoric and the practice of slavery, to most whites of the time "people" meant "whites." The Constitution was a conservative document, a compact between the northern bourgeoisie and the southern slave-owning aristocracy. The economic life of the infant republic was so heavily dependent on slavery and the slave trade that most whites in the North as well as in the South regarded abolitionism as irresponsible and mischievous radicalism, much in the same way that their descendants later anathematized Socialism and Communism.

The Negro was defined as a subhuman, disfranchised part of the polity, as a special form of chattel, assessed at three fifths of a man by Constitutional compromise between South and North. The Indian groups with which the settlers clashed on the ever-expanding frontier were first treated as alien nations who could be either enemies or allies against competing European powers; later as a nuisance and an impediment to white expansion which had to be exterminated or pushed back; still later, as shiftless beggars and irresponsible wards of the republic; and only belatedly as fellow citizens. We may find ironic symbolism in the fact that the hallowed bell, which was to "Proclaim Liberty throughout all the land unto all the inhabitants thereof," cracked during its testing in 1752, was recast, cracked once more in 1835, and has remained in that condition ever since. Perhaps it was the bell's way of saying "I cannot tell a lie."

Myrdal's main theme is that one of the most important forces for change in American race relations is the guilt or at least discomfort of most members of the dominant group over the discrepancy between the "American Creed" and the treatment of the Negro [2]. Whatever the situation may have been during the last two or three decades, and notwithstanding some soul-searching by a few genteel slave-owning intellectuals like Jefferson and Madison in the late eighteenth and early nineteenth centuries, there is little evidence of an "American Dilemma" during most of the nineteenth century and the first third of the twentieth century. The democratic, egalitarian, and libertarian ideals were reconciled with slavery and genocide by restricting the definition of humanity to whites. Thus Chief Justice Roger Brooke Taney concluded in his famous Dred Scott decision of 1857 that he had no ground to assert that Negroes were not "beings of an inferior order . . . so far inferior that they had no rights which the white man was bound to respect." Abraham Lincoln who, contrary to all evidence, has been immortalized as the "Great Emancipator," was offended when he was accused of abolitionism and emphatically declared in 1858 during the Lincoln-Douglas debates:

"I am not, nor ever have been in favor of bringing about in any way the social and political equality of the white and black races; I am not, nor ever have been, in favor of making voters or jurors of Negroes, nor qualifying them to hold office . . . I will say in addition to this that there is a physical difference between the white and black races which I believe will ever forbid the two races living together on terms of social and political equality. And in as much as they cannot so live, while they do remain together, there must be the position of superior and inferior, and I as much as any other man am in favor of having the superior position assigned to the white race."

Through a revealing twist of mind the Pennsylvania-born James Buchanan eloquently defended slavery on grounds of the people's freedom of self-determination and of the sacredness of private property and the Constitution. Even a man of Jefferson's intellectual stature made numerous racist statements concerning Negroes, though he wavered between racism and environmentalism [3].

Apart from American Indians, and later a number of nonwhite immigrants such as Mexicans, Puerto Ricans, Chinese and Japanese, United States society has been divided into two major racial castes—Negroes and whites. Negroes have been defined traditionally as all persons with any black African ancestry who cannot "pass" as whites. In the *ante bellum* period the most common form of contact between whites and Negroes, indeed that which molded the entire pattern of race relations, took place on the slave plantations of the Black Belt of the South. Slavery was not restricted to the southern states; it existed on a smaller scale outside the South until the Civil War. (The 1860 Census lists 18 slaves in the northeastern region and 29 in the West. The Middle Atlantic states had slave holdings numbering in the tens of thousands until the 1820s when New York abolished slavery.) Similarly, not all Negroes were slaves, but the vast majority was. In 1860 on the eve of the Civil War, some 4.44

RACE AND RACISM

TABLE 4.1
United States Population by Race (1790-1960)

Year	Per cent White	Per cent Negro	Per cent Other Nonwhite	Total in Thousands
1790	80.73	19.27	N.A.	3,929
1800	81.22	18.88	N.A.	5,308
1810	80.97	19.03	N.A.	7,240
1820	81.61	18.39	N.A.	9,638
1830	81.90	18.10	N.A.	12,866
1840	83.16	16.84	N.A.	17,069
1850	84.31	15.69	N.A.	23,192
1860	85.62	14.13	0.25	31,443
1870	87.11	12.66	0.23	38,558
1880	86.54	13.12	0.34	50,156
1890	87.53	11.90	0.57	62,948
1900	87.92	11.62	0.46	75,995
1910	88.86	10.69	0.45	91,972
1920	89.70	9.90	0.40	105,710
1930	89.82	9.69	0.49	122,775
1940	89.78	9.77	0.45	131,669
1950	89.55	9.98	0.47	150,697
1960	88.58	10.52	0.90*	179,323

* Includes Alaska and Hawaii.

millions in a total population of 31.44 millions were Negroes, and only some 488,000 were free. Some 47 per cent of the free Negroes lived outside the South. Some of the slaves worked in cities as craftsmen or domestic servants; but the plantation based on the monoculture, first of tobacco in Virginia and later of cotton throughout the Black Belt, was the involuntary home of the mass of Negro Americans.

The slavery regime of the South, although much harsher than that of Brazil, showed a great many structural characteristics in common with it [4]. The plantation was largely an autonomous microcosm in which masters and slaves lived in close symbiosis. The slave owners constituted for the most part a feudal, land-owning aristocracy that dominated both the economic and the political life of the South, and indeed to a considerable extent of the nation. (Ten of the sixteen presidents elected before the

Civil War were born in the South and as many were slave owners.) Slave owners comprised only a small minority of the white population; in 1860 there were around 350,000 slave owners, that is, about 1.3 per cent of the country's whites. The high and steadily rising value of slaves (by the end of the slavery era, a healthy young man was worth around $2000) limited slave ownership to the wealthy.

The small world of the plantation was rigidly stratified. An elaborate etiquette of race relations regulated interaction between master and slave. Slaves were expected to behave submissively through self-deprecatory gestures and speech, the frequent use of terms of respect toward whites, self-debasing clowning, and general fulfillment of their role expectation as incompetent and backward grown-up children. Conversely, masters addressed slaves familiarly by their first names, sometimes preceded by the term "uncle" or "aunt" with old family retainers. The owner's family lived in the big house in close physical proximity with the slave "elite" of house servants (chambermaids, cooks, butlers, coachmen, and nursemaids). Whites and Negroes grew up and played together as children; white infants were breast-fed and raised by black "mammies"; adolescent boys often had their first sexual experience with a slave and usually continued to have Negro concubines throughout their sexually active lifetimes. Miscegenation in the form of concubinage between white men and Negro women was accepted and was quite frequent, particularly between house slaves and their masters. Intermarriage was outlawed in most states and sexual relations between white women and Negro men were strongly condemned, but the other form of concubinage was an aspect of the general exploitation that was inherent in slavery.

The mass of unskilled field hands who were at the bottom of the slave hierarchy did not have as close contact with their owners as the house slaves. They lived in the slave barracks and rarely entered the big house; they interacted mostly with the plantation overseers who were often recruited from the poor white class of small farmers. Most of the few free Negroes who lived in the South were craftsmen or domestic servants, and their economic status, though higher than that of most field hands, was not substantially different from that of house slaves. Politically and legally, they were subjected to numerous disabilities in the North as well as the South [5].

Stereotypes of whites concerning Negroes conformed to the paternalistic model of race relations. Negroes were regarded as immature, irresponsible, unintelligent, physically strong, happy-go-lucky, musically gifted, grown-up children. They were treated at best like a "stern but just" father would deal with backward children, at worst like special and expensive species of livestock whose labor was to be exploited for the greatest economic gain. Although, of course, slave owners were by nature neither more nor less depraved than any other human group, the United States variety of chattel slavery was one of the harshest in the world. Both church and state did little to interfere with the arbitrary power of the master over his human property, short of homicide. Not only did the slave have little legal recourse and standing but also the law buttressed slavery and successfully hindered emancipation by such devices as requiring the master to post a bond when manumitting a slave. Far from increasing over time, the proportion of free Negroes steadily declined from 18.8 per cent of the total Negro population in 1820 to 11.0 per cent in 1860. Most religious denominations sought Biblical rationalizations for the "peculiar institution" and did little to encourage baptism and marriage of slaves. Stable family life among slaves was impossible; even common law unions were frequently broken up by separate sale of partners; children above infancy were often separated from their mothers; and Negro women were constantly at the sexual disposal of their masters and their overseers. Even a century after emancipation the disruptive heritage of slavery in the most basic of all social groups, the nuclear family, is still profoundly felt and results in high illegitimacy rates and what Frazier called the "matrifocal" family [6].

Not unexpectedly there were a number of slave revolts, of which the most notorious was the Nat Turner Rebellion of 1831. All of them, however, were quite limited and localized in scope and never came close to being successful, even temporarily. The constant fear by southern whites of a general slave uprising in the United States was certainly out of proportion with the actual danger, although the successful Haitian example lent some basis of plausibility to the fear. In fact, however, American slavery was such a shattering and dehumanizing institution that the Negroes were far too atomized and too geographically isolated on the various plantations for concerted collective action.

In addition, slavery brought about the virtually complete deculturation of Afro-Americans. Even though Negroes constituted up to 20 per cent of the population in the early days of the republic, they left hardly a trace of African culture on American soil. The wide variety of ethnic groups from which Afro-Americans came, the trauma of the "Middle Passage," the months spent in transit in slave depots, the dispersion and intermixture with whites and American-born slaves, and the destruction of family life were among the main factors contributive to the rapid cultural assimilation of Negroes with the dominant group. Along with this process of deculturation and acculturation, Negro slaves adopted to a large degree the values and attitudes of the whites to the extent of internalizing the feeling of their own social and "racial" inferiority. This "brainwashing" was so successful that many Negroes came to accept their status as inescapable and in some cases even developed feelings of affection and loyalty toward their masters.

Even today, a century after the abolition of slavery, self-deprecation, collective inferiority feelings, emulation of white standards and values, and compensatory phenomena are still evident among some Negro Americans [7]. To cite but one illustration, vast sums are spent by Negroes on hair-straighteners, skin-bleachers, and other cosmetics to make them resemble the dominant group more closely. (Consciously, the motivation is seldom that they want to look white, but rather that they have so profoundly internalized the esthetic biases of the dominant group that they identify straight hair and light skin with "beauty." Thus what is narcissism for the whites becomes ego-destroying self-hatred for Negroes.) There is little question that the ruthlessness and the thorough cultural disruption of United States slavery robbed a great many slaves of their self-respect, and hence that the social system of the ante-bellum South rested not only on coercion but also to a great measure on the sullen consent or acquiescence that accompanies conditions of extreme degradation [8]. Chattel slavery was, of course, dehumanizing not only for the Negroes but also for the whites.

A greater amount of blatantly racist and partisan literature has probably been written about the Civil War and the Reconstruction era than about any other period in American history [9]. Nevertheless, a number of the contentions made in accounts sympathetic to the Confederacy are closer to the truth than the quasi-official version which resulted from the *ex post facto* prettifying process of "liberal" historians. Although the long-standing conflict over the *extension* of slavery was important in bringing about the Civil War, the latter was obviously not fought to free the slaves. The Emancipation Proclamation of 1863 was largely a tactical maneuver issued in spite of Lincoln's considerable misgivings and a result of considerable pressure from Union Army generals who felt that it would deal the Confederacy a serious blow. Interestingly, it was carefully designed not to emancipate, in fact, a single slave; it excluded not only the slave-owning border states who fought on the Union side but also those districts of the Confederacy under Union Army occupation. Thus the Proclamation applied only to those areas in which it patently could not be enforced.

The Reconstruction period (which lasted until 1877 if one takes the "Compromise" and the withdrawal of Federal military occupation from the last of the former Confederate states as the criterion) was the closest the United States came to a social revolution. True enough, much of the program of the Radical Republicans was motivated more by a desire to smash the power of the old Bourbon aristocracy of the South than by pro-Negro considerations. The most that can be said is that Reconstruction was a complex mixture of vindictiveness, opportunism, and humanitarianism, and that racism was fully as prevalent in the North as in the South, even among "liberals." But the motivations of the Radicals are in the last analysis of little relevance; the fact is that the short-range accomplishments of Reconstruction were considerable. The economic basis of the old southern aristocracy was destroyed; slavery was abolished; a (segregated) school system was established to educate the freedmen; a number of freedmen were given land; within a few years Negroes were given the right to vote, both *de jure* and *de facto,* and were elected to important positions in state and federal governments. Between 1869 and 1876 two Negro senators and fourteen representatives were elected to the United States Congress, a record which has not since been equaled. By 1870 the Freedmen's Bureau had established more than 4200 schools with some 9300 teachers and 247,000 pupils [10].

In short, Reconstruction shook the very foundations of the old South and for a period threw it in truly revolutionary turmoil. A century later we are painfully trying to recapture the gains achieved temporarily during Reconstruction, and we are still falling short of them in the political sphere. Why then did Reconstruction eventually fail, and how did the counter-revolution succeed in re-establishing white supremacy on a new basis in the South? Reconstruction failed largely because it was a "revolution from the top," directed by a segment of the dominant group (the Radical Republicans with the help of the Federal Army), with little active support and push from the masses of the freedmen. Obviously, this is not to imply that most Negroes did not welcome the demise of slavery and that significant numbers of individual Negroes did not play important, indeed distinguished, roles in the various Reconstruction regimes of the South. Du Bois has conclusively shown that a number of Negroes were not passive recipients of the blessings of Reconstruction but active participants in it. It remains true, however, that Negroes were "junior partners" in the revolution and that the mass of Negroes was too atomized, politically untrained, and unorganized to constitute an independent political force in the South.

The aftermath of the Civil War marked an abrupt change from a paternalistic to a competitive type of race relations, partly as a result of the disruption which followed the defeat of the Confederacy and partly as a consequence of wider and more profound transformations which affected the entire country. The old agrarian, feudal world of the slave plantation was destroyed, and with it the traditional master-servant model of race relations. Freed Negroes migrated in great numbers to the cities of the South, and to a lesser extent outside the South, and entered for the first time in direct competition on the labor market with the poor white farmers of the South and the urban white working class of both the North and the South.

Several trends, which began to manifest themselves on a large scale at the time of the Civil War or just before, made the second half of the nineteenth century the most dynamic period in United States history and exacerbated racial competition. The two years preceding the mid-century marked the beginning of two momentous events and the end of a third one. The California gold rush was the final phase of the territorial expansion of the United States by a process of land encroachment and frontier wars between white settlers and a number of small Indian groups. It took several more decades to beat the last remnants of the indigenous population into total submission and to reduce the last Indian lands to the status of human zoos for the amusement of tourists and the delight of anthropologists. However, by 1850 the Pacific Ocean had become the western frontier of the United States. The war of conquest against Mexico marked the beginning of the United States as the great imperialist power in the Western Hemisphere and almost gave the United States its present continental frontiers. Finally, the Irish potato famine triggered off the mass immigration of Europeans in response to the rising demand for industrial labor. Through European immigration the nonwhite population was gradually reduced to 10 per cent of the total.

The immediate pre-Civil War era also marked the massive development of heavy iron and steel industry, and of railway transportation, and the early phase in the growth of monopoly capitalism. The United States was in the process of becoming the first major non-European industrial power. Indeed, the Civil War was the first major conflict in the world in which warfare itself could be described as largely industrialized. Rapid urbanization, the mushrooming of working class slums, high unemployment, massive internal migration, and all the disruptive forces and conflicts of early capitalism contributed to the complete change in patterns of race relations and to a steadily rising tide of racial, ethnic, and religious bigotry.

Ideologically, the last third of the nineteenth century was characterized by a syndrome of *laissez-faire* capitalism in the economic sphere, of jingoism and imperialism in foreign relations, and of racial and ethnic intolerance in the domestic social sphere. The writings of Theodore Roosevelt and of other American racists like Madison Grant and Charles Carrol epitomize this era which could be termed the Golden Age of Racism. Social Darwinism and economic liberalism were fused to rationalize the survival of the wealthiest in the industrial jungle and to give racism the accolade of Science [11]. Negroes were not the sole victims, of course. Anti-Oriental agitation was rampant on the West Coast; anti-Semitism and anti-Catholic pogroms swept the large cities of the East; the Know-Nothings rivaled in xenophobia and ethnocentrism with the Ku Klux Klan [12], but Negroes, being the largest and most visible group, bore the brunt of the new competitive form of prejudice that was flourishing.

More specifically, as the old system of agrarian paternalism was breaking down, new forms of oppression and exploitation were being developed to keep the Negro "in his place," and to maintain white supremacy. A number of paternalistic remnants such as the ante-bellum racial etiquette still linger on in the rural Black Belt [13]. However, starting in 1865, a new phase of race relations began, and new white attitudes toward Negroes developed. The sterotype of the "happy singing slave" gave way to that of the "uppity," "insolent," "pushy" Negro who did not know his place, who was out to compete with the white workers and to rape white women. Anti-Negro prejudice became heavily laden with sexuality; the already complex mythology of Negro sexual potency and eroticism and of the purity of the white woman was developed further; phobia of miscegenation grew; and interracial concubinage between white men and Negro women became more clandestine, more commercialized, and probably less fertile as well as less common [14].

In the economic sphere slavery gave way to share-cropping and debt peonage. After an initial exodus to the towns, many freedmen had to return to the land to find a basis of subsistence. The plantation owners broke up their lands into small plots to be cultivated by individual tenants. The slave barracks near the big house gave way to a pattern of dispersed wooden shacks. Money lending, or rather the loan of food, seeds, tools, and other necessities to be charged at arbitrary prices against the value of the tenant's share of the crop, became an economic substitute for slavery. Through perpetual indebtedness, the tenant farmer was nearly as securely tied to the land and to his landlord as he was under slavery.

More important yet were the political and social aspects of the counter-revolution that followed Reconstruction. Interestingly, this counter-revolution did not set in immediately after the withdrawal of Federal troops. As shown by C. Vann Woodward, it did not gain momentum until about 1890, because in the interim period the old aristocracy attempted to maintain its power in southern states by manipulating the Negro vote against the poor whites [15]. With the demise of these Bourbon regimes and the rise of *Herrenvolk* democracy in the South, a whole set of new mechanisms for the repression of Negroes was instituted. Among the first measures were a number of state laws aimed at nullifying the effect of the Fifteenth Amendment. Since Negroes could not be deprived of the right to vote on grounds of race, a whole battery of literacy and educational tests, poll taxes, "white primaries," and "grandfather clauses" was developed to achieve the same result. In a few years the overwhelming mass of Southern Negroes had lost its franchise rights and was not to begin regaining them until after World War II. Indeed, we have yet fully to regain the achievements of Reconstruction in Negro voting and representation.

Disfranchisement was, however, only one prong of the trident used to put the Negro back "in his place." The second one was "Jim Crow," as physical segregation by race became known in the South. Segregation was, of course, not entirely new in the South; but what there was of it before the Civil War was the ecological and geographical expression of the distribution of slaves (in the Black Belt and in the *upper* class districts of old southern towns) rather than a mechanism of white domination. In fact, such ante-bellum segregation as existed was more along class than along racial lines. The mass of Negroes had little contact with the mass of whites, but the house servants lived in close symbiosis with their masters. There was little racial segregation for its own sake. Indeed, as I have suggested earlier, the elaborate mechanisms of *social* distance which existed under slavery left status inequality unthreatened, hence made segregation "unnecessary."

In spite of hygienic and moral rationalizations for Jim Crow after Reconstruction, whites, and particularly southern whites, continued to accept intimate contact with Negroes, provided it clearly took place in a situation of unequal status (e.g., between employer and employee, or master and servant). However, the abolition of slavery, rapid urbanization and industrialization, great geographical mobility, and other dynamic factors undermined the old mechanisms of caste distance and the entire fabric of paternalistic subordination of the Negro. The diffuse, intimate, noncompetitive, complementary, asymmetrical, particularistic, holistic roles that characterized Negro-white interaction were replaced by segmental, impersonal, competitive, and potentially symmetrical and universalistic relationships. The white farmers and workers (both indigenous and immigrant) were suddenly threatened by equal status contact with the mass of Negroes. To forestall this possibility and to replace the increasingly inappropriate and obsolete mechanisms of social distance which had regulated the interaction of the Bourbon aristocracy with their slaves, racial segregation was increasingly resorted to as a second line of defense for maintaining white supremacy.

Segregation was no longer simply an ecological correlate of the economic and social class system, but a calculated, invidious device of racial subordination. The monoracial urban ghetto with its set of duplicatory institutions (churches, schools, theaters, shops, professional services) became a socially and economically self-contained microcosm and replaced the biracial plantation or the urban mansion with its backyard servant quarters. Structurally, roles and institutions, which had hitherto been characterized by racial *complementarity* (e.g., in the division of labor), became increasingly *duplicatory*. Next to the dominant structure of the "white world" a subordinate but parallel Negro *Lumpenstruktur* developed, complete with its make-believe pseudo-bourgeoisie, its powerless pseudo-elite, and its debutante balls [16]. Racial segregation, to which the Supreme Court soon gave its blessing in its famous "separate but equal" doctrine propounded in the Plessy versus Ferguson decision of 1896, became a consuming monomania of whites. In the South, it was enforced through a multitude of laws and customs providing for separate and unequal (or nonexistent for Negroes) facilities in virtually every sphere of life. It became a punishable offense against the laws or the mores for whites and Negroes to travel, eat, defecate, wait, be buried, make love, play, relax, and even speak together, except in the stereo- typed context of master and servant interaction. In the North, segregation was to a greater extent extra-legal, and outside the monolithic ghettoes with their separate institutional structure, it took a less blatantly visible form, but it was only slightly less rigid.

The third prong of the counter-revolutionary trident was the development of new terrorist tactics to supplement the other mechanisms of racial subordination. Secret organizations such as the Ku Klux Klan resorted to intimidation, brutality, and murder as their major means for keeping Negroes and "nigger-lovers" in their place, but so did spontaneous groups of unorganized private citizens as well as the police, which, in the South, has traditionally played the role of uniformed vigilantes in the service of the dominant whites. The most notorious and extreme form of ter- rorism was lynching, but other tactics were also used such as beatings, cross-burnings, masked night rides through Negro dis- tricts, verbal threats, hate rallies, public humiliations, and ran- dom discharging of shotguns in windows.

Lynching is difficult to define, because at the limit it can be- come synonymous with homicide. Here we shall define it as illegal homicide committed by one or more persons who are not regarded by most members of the dominant group in the local community as criminals, and whose intention is not only to punish the victim (who may, in fact, be known to be innocent of any crime) but also to exercise social control when the legal machinery is regarded as inadequate. In this sense, lynching existed before the Civil War, but it was overwhelmingly an act of whites against whites in attempting to control frontier lawlessness, where legal machinery was either absent or ineffective. After the Civil War, lynching assumed a different character. It became a racial phe- nomenon: most victims were Negroes and most criminals were whites; it was no longer a device to control banditry in an an- archistic frontier, but rather a terrorist technique to maintain white supremacy in settled communities with an established legal order.

Two different subtypes of racial lynching can be distinguished. The "mob" or "proletarian" lynching assumed the character of a highly ritualized mass orgy of sadism which included torture, burning, castration, and the carving of "souvenirs" from the victim's clothing or body. Often the victim was not guilty of any crime or guilty simply of a breach of etiquette. In contrast to "mob" lynching, "Bourbon" lynching was engaged in by a few pillars of the community who, having made some attempt to ascertain the guilt of the victim, killed him expeditiously, usually by shooting and without publicity. During the decade after the Civil War alone an estimated 3500 Negroes were lynched. With the advent of the twentieth century there was a fairly steady decline in the incidence of lynchings, but, contrary to frequent statements, lynchings have not disappeared, except through a bit of semantic prestidigitation. Recent murders of civil rights workers are curiously not referred to as lynchings, perhaps to salvage the propaganda myth that lynching belongs to the past.

World War I marked the first indications of new changes in race relations. As a response to demand for labor and industrial expansion in the North, Negro emigration from the South accelerated, thereby scattering the nonwhite minority more and more widely over the nation and correspondingly reducing the Negro percentage in the South. In 1910, 89 per cent of the Negroes lived in the South and 30 per cent of the Southern population were Negroes. By 1930 these percentages had dropped to 79 and 25 per cent (see Table 4.2). Negro migration was also a process of increasing urbanization in both the South and the non-South. In summary, the Negro population left the rural Black Belt to

TABLE 4.2
Negro Population of the United States (1900–1960)

Year	Percentage of Negroes Living in South	Negro Percentage of Southern Population
1900	89.69	32.31
1910	89.04	29.77
1920	84.18	26.90
1930	78.73	24.73
1940	76.99	23.77
1950	67.98	21.66
1960	60.92	20.91

populate the widely dispersed urban ghettoes of large metropolitan centers where they displaced as unskilled workers the European immigrants. World War I also exposed hundreds of thousands of Negro soldiers to conditions outside the South and overseas, and "uppity" returning veterans aroused mounting hostility from whites after the war, as shown by a wave of race riots and a temporary rise in the number of lynchings.

By the 1930s a few judicial decisions began to nibble at the edifice of racial segregation, and both the Great Depression and the New Deal policies exercised a certain leveling effect between poor whites and poor Negroes. Migration outside the South continued, if only in search of nondiscriminatory relief. However, it took World War II to unleash forces powerful enough to undermine the racial status quo. Negro migration to the large industrial centers of the North, the Great Lakes, and as far as the West Coast greatly accelerated during the war and continued thereafter. By 1960 only 61 per cent of Negroes were living in the South and only 21 per cent of the southern population were Negro (see Table 4.2). More servicemen than ever before fought and lived abroad, albeit in a Jim Crow army, and came in contact with societies in which racial bigotry did not exist. The strong incentive not to waste manpower motivated the establishment of Fair Employment Practices Commissions and opened up new occupational opportunities for Negroes. Racism, of course, was far from dead, as shown by the wartime internment of United States citizens of Japanese descent condoned by Franklin D. Roosevelt.

The major landmarks of the history of postwar desegregation, such as the 1948 integration of the Armed Forces, the 1954 Supreme Court decision on the integration of public schools, and the Montgomery bus boycott, are too well known to need reiterating here [17]. Suffice it to say that the amount of progress realized to date warrants neither the optimism nor the complacency which, until the last three or four years, was fashionable among "liberal" intellectuals and social scientists. The objective situation has improved, to be sure, but the change is impressive only by conservative standards.

Recent developments seem to highlight two points. First, with the "revolution of rising expectations" on the part of Negro Americans, the gap between reality and aspirations has increased in spite of progress; consequently, the level of racial conflict, of frustration, and of alienation has risen in the past few years. The present situation is probably more explosive than ever before. Second, the real progress which has been made in the past seven years is the result of mass militancy and of the adoption of unconventional methods of protest such as passive resistance and civil disobedience by the oppressed minorities, rather than of magnanimity and benevolence from the Federal government or the dominant group at large.

Yet, can one speak of a "Negro revolution"? The answer is clearly "no," or at least "not yet." All the major civil rights groups (N.A.A.C.P., Urban League, C.O.R.E., Student Non-Violent Coordinating Committee, Southern Christian Leadership Conference) are reform movements in the sense that, far from questioning the underlying values and premises of American society, they seek legitimacy in the American Creed and Christian ethics and plead for a change of practices in line with the dominant group ideology [18]. These movements have so far done little more than call the bluff of nearly 200 years of democratic rhetoric in the face of actual exploitation and oppression. If anything, the very respectability of civil rights as a protest cause probably deflects the attention of many people from many more fundamental problems such as the creative use of leisure, automation, the distribution of social rewards, the oligarchic exercise of power, militarism, and the ownership and control of means of production.

Many well-meaning American "liberals" mistakingly regard racism as the underlying cause of most evils in their society, instead of viewing it as but a fairly superficial symptom of much more widespread and basic problems. (Thus racial discrimination in housing is almost impossible to abolish effectively under a system that allows unlimited individual ownership of real estate and private control of the housing market.) Many "liberals" see a panacea in "whitewashing" their black fellow countrymen; they conceive of the struggle for the abolition of racial discrimination as a process of "bourgeoisification" of America.

Broadly speaking, ideological and political developments in the United States can take, it seems to me, two directions. Indeed, the present civil rights conflict has simultaneously activated and exacerbated both of these tendencies. On the one hand, there can be a generalized political radicalization of American society along socialist or "new left" lines, with the clear realization that race is an epiphenomenon devoid of intrinsic significance and that present conflicts and problems transcend race. (The "Great Society" program seems a timid attempt to graft some aspects of new left ideology onto old-fashioned liberalism, but the radical left is still very much a voice in the wilderness.)

The other alternative, of course, is militant black separatism, such as cropped up in both religious and secular versions. For demographic if for no other reasons black separatism does not have much of a long-range future, but its potential for short-range chaos is impressive.

Pluralism and even separatism can be viable policy alternatives if a group meets certain conditions of relative size, geographical concentration, economic self-sufficiency, and cultural distinctiveness and autonomy. Beyond the specific stigma of skin pigmentation and its numerous social and psychological consequences, Negro Americans have virtually nothing more in common than they do with any other Americans; and stigmatization itself, of course, is far from being a Negro monopoly. Surely a stigma can never be the basis of a program; it can at best become a slogan. It is easy enough to understand how the folly of white segregation generates the counterfolly of black separatism, but the prospect is not very appealing. The United States is now in the ironic situation of seeing integration ideology change camps as the country painfully gropes toward a resolution of social conflicts. Let us hope that the integrationists are not going to be defined as the next generation of Uncle Toms.

NOTES

[1] For a recent statement that is generally congruent with my own position see Eli Ginzberg and Alfred S. Eichner, *The Troublesome Presence*. See also Thomas F. Gossett, *Race, The History of an Idea in America*.

[2] Gunnar Myrdal, *An American Dilemma*.

[3] In an unpublished study of racial attitudes of American Presidents, I found that, with the exception of the two Adamses and Garfield, all presidents openly expressed racial prejudice in and out of office until the 1950s. Some like Jackson and Theodore Roosevelt were even virulent

bigots, although most of them simply reflected majority attitudes. The only president to emerge as distinctly antiracist and fully "modern" in his outlook on race was John Quincy Adams.

[4] For sociological and historical accounts of slavery see Kenneth M. Stampp, *The Peculiar Institution;* Frederick L. Olmsted, *The Slave States;* Stanley M. Elkins, *Slavery;* Ulrich B. Phillips, *Life and Labor in the Old South;* and John Hope Franklin, *From Slavery to Freedom.*

[5] Leon F. Litwack documents the status of free Negroes outside the South in his book *North of Slavery.*

[6] E. Franklin Frazier, *The Negro in the United States,* and *The Negro Family in the United States.*

[7] In his polemical book *Black Bourgeoisie,* E. Franklin Frazier bitterly attacked these traits among the Negro middle class.

[8] The Nazi concentration camps provide us with more recent examples of similar phenomena. European colonial regimes in Africa also present some similarities but in a much milder form, because in Africa the Europeans seldom succeeded in destroying indigenous cultures (except among the Hottentots in the Western Cape). See my article "Racialism and Assimilation in Africa and the Americas."

[9] Notable exceptions are W. E. B. Du Bois' *Black Reconstruction,* and more recently C. Vann Woodward, *The Strange Career of Jim Crow.*

[10] W. E. B. Du Bois, *op. cit.,* p. 648.

[11] Thomas F. Gossett, *Race, The History of an Idea in America.*

[12] For accounts of ethnic prejudice see Oscar Handlin, *Race and Nationality in American Life;* and Gustavus Myers, *History of Bigotry in the United States.*

[13] Cf. John Dollard, *Caste and Class in a Southern Town;* Allison Davis, B. B. Gardner, and M. R. Gardner, *Deep South;* Bertram W. Doyle, *The Etiquette of Race Relations in the South;* and Charles S. Johnson, *Shadow of the Plantation.*

[14] One of the best psychoanalytic interpretations of race relations in the South can be found in Lillian Smith, *Killers of the Dream.*

[15] Cf. *The Strange Career of Jim Crow.*

[16] Frazier's *Black Bourgeoisie* remains the classic statement of this phenomenon.

[17] Among over a score of recent surveys and accounts of recent race relations research and of the desegregation process, see Milton M. Gordon, *Assimilation in American Life;* Thomas F. Pettigrew, *A Profile of the Negro American;* Peter I. Rose, *They and We;* Charles E. Silberman, *Crisis in Black and White;* James W. Vander Zanden, *American Minority Relations;* and J. Milton Yinger, *A Minority Group in American Society.* The results of a large-scale and recent study of United States race relations are reported in Robin Williams, *Strangers Next Door.*

[18] The recent evolution of the SNCC under the leadership of Stokely Carmichael represents a partial departure from the ideological premises of the dominant group.

V

South Africa

If racism is an endemic disease in the United States, in South Africa it has become a way of life. Of all contemporary multiracial societies, South Africa is the most complexly and rigidly stratified on the basis of race, the one in which race has greatest salience *vis à vis* other structural principles, and the one which is most ridden with conflict and internal contradictions [1].

The "white problem" of South Africa began in 1652 with the establishment by the Dutch East India Company of a refreshing station for its Asia-bound vessels at the Cape of Good Hope. The local population of what is now the western part of the Cape Province consisted of sparsely settled Hottentot pastoralists and Bushmen hunters and gatherers. At first race was not the basis for status differentiation between Europeans and indigenous people. Religion was the important criterion and baptism conferred legal and, to a considerable extent, social equality with the Dutch settlers. During the first years of Dutch settlement there were a few instances of Christian marriage between Dutchmen and Hottentot women.

Within a generation, however, color or race had supplanted religion as a criterion of membership in the dominant group, and by the end of the seventeenth century a rigid system of racial stratification existed at the Cape. In 1658 the first shipload of

slaves entered Cape Town in response to the white settlers'
clamor for servile help and to the scarcity and unreliability of the
indigenous population for this purpose. The slave society of the
Cape remained much more restricted in both area and number of
people than that of the United States, Brazil, or even Mexico [2].
Slavery was almost entirely confined to the towns and the settled
agricultural districts of the Western Cape (i.e., to Cape Town
and the surrounding towns of Stellenbosch, Paarl, and Swellen-
dam with their rural hinterland of vineyards, fruit orchards, and
wheat fields). In 1700 the settlement consisted of only 1308 whites
and 838 slaves; by 1805 it had grown to 25,757 whites, 29,545
slaves, and an estimated 28,000 Hottentots. Slaves came mostly
from eastern Africa, Madagascar, and to a lesser extent from the
Dutch East Indies. In 1795 Britain took over the Cape Colony
(ceding it briefly again to Holland from 1803 to 1806) and in
1834 abolished slavery throughout her Empire.

The slave society of the Cape was not based on monoculture
and on large plantations, but rather on medium-sized farms
engaging in fairly diversified cash agriculture. It did, however,
exhibit most characteristics of a paternalistic type of race relations, and showed many resemblances with the slave systems of
the New World. The white farmer living on his autonomous
estate constituted with his family and his retinue of slaves a large
patriarchal unit in daily and intimate contact. The familiar pattern of the big house and the adjacent slave quarters was common,
though in some cases slaves even lived in the basement of the big
house. House slaves and skilled craftsmen who interbred extensively with their masters constituted a slave elite compared to
the mass of field hands and to the "public" slaves owned by the
Dutch East India Company. Masters and house slaves lived together in the big house, played together as children, and prayed
and fornicated together as adults.

Spatial segregation was minimal, and what there was of it was
dictated by the dominant group's convenience and desire for
privacy, rather than as a mechanism of social control. Unequal
status was symbolized and maintained through an elaborate
etiquette of race relations and through sumptuary regulations, in
short through mechanisms of *social* distance. A number of Dutch
terms of reference and address (some of which have survived in

modern Afrikaans) designate various sex and age statuses within both the dominant and the subordinate groups (e.g., *pay, jong, hotnot, booi, outa, aia, meid, skepsels, kleinjong, klonkie, baas, witman, nooi, and seur*) and testify to a complex racial etiquette. When going to church, prosperous Dutch matrons were followed by a procession of slaves, one carrying their umbrella, another their prayer book, a third their footwarmer or *stoofje*. Slaves were forbidden to walk in the streets with a lighted pipe or to wear shoes, for these objects were regarded as symbols of free status.

Miscegenation in the form of concubinage between Dutch men and slave and Hottentot women was quite common and no stigma was attached to it. Dutch boys frequently had their first sexual experiences with slave girls. The East India Company condoned the use of its slave lodge in Cape Town as a notorious brothel for sailors and soldiers. (Curiously, it imposed a 9 P.M. curfew, perhaps more to keep their slaves fit for work than out of a sense of propriety.) The product of this extensive miscegenation between Dutchmen, slaves, and free men of color, such as Hottentots and Malay political exiles from the East Indies, gave rise to the people now referred to as Cape Coloureds and who today are half as numerous as the whites, even though a great many light Coloureds have "passed" into the white group.

The division of labor was clearly along racial lines, manual work being regarded as degrading by the whites and engaged in almost solely by slaves and Hottentots. Although there were some white craftsmen, they were in effect shop owners supervising colored labor. Roles and statuses were unambiguously determined by race more than by any other criterion. Manumission was relatively infrequent (between 1715 and 1792, for example, there were only 893 cases in a slave population that grew from more than 2000 to nearly 15,000) and did not confer many privileges to the free person of color over the slave. Hottentots, although nominally free, lost both their pasture land and their cattle to the encroaching whites and thus were soon reduced to a condition of serfdom. Free people of color were subject to vagrancy laws and master-and-servant laws which greatly restricted their mobility and reduced them to a state of symbiotic dependence on the Dutch settlers that differed little from slavery.

Contrasted with the settled region around Cape Town in the

Western Cape were the frontier districts into which the trekboers ("traveling peasants") continuously expanded in search of new pastures and cattle to trade or steal from the Hottentot and Bantu. "Trekking" began in the late seventeenth century and reached a climax in the Great Trek that started in 1836 and continued for a decade. The Boers (as the Dutch semi-nomads came to be known) were for the most part poorer farmers or younger sons who did not inherit land in the settled districts of the Cape; they expanded to the North, especially to the Northeast along the coast, pushing farther and farther from the Cape as their sheep and cattle depleted the pastures. Until the 1770s they encountered mostly Hottentots and Bushmen on whose lands they encroached.

The Boers carried out a policy of genocide against the Bushmen, whom they hunted down in organized commandoes and whom they exterminated in the present area of South Africa. The Hottentots, who were pastoralists, had cattle and their skills as herdsmen to offer the Boers. In spite of a number of frontier skirmishes and cattle raids between them, the Hottentots were not wiped out. After they lost their pastures and cattle, they became herdsmen and servants to the Boers, with whom they eventually miscegenated themselves out of existence to give rise to a group of Coloureds known as "Bastards" [3]. The relationship prevailing between the Boers and their Hottentot serfs was a rugged, frontier variety of paternalism. Contrary to the settled districts around Cape Town, where the whites relied mostly on slave labor, the frontier Boers were usually too poor to own slaves, and they depended almost solely on Hottentot labor. They regarded the Hottentots as slothful, unintelligent, and irresponsible. Yet contact between masters and servants was very close, and the style of life of the Boers living in temporary thatched huts was not appreciably different from that of the indigenous nomads.

Beginning in the 1770s Boer expansion was virtually stopped for over half a century at the Great Fish River when the whites encountered the Bantu-speaking nations who were in the process of migrating southward. The Bantu groups (whose descendants now comprise over two thirds of South Africa's population and call themselves "Africans") were organized in centralized states numbering hundreds of thousands of fairly densely settled people. The Bantu proved a much more formidable opponent than the Hottentots and Bushmen, and a whole series of frontier wars and cattle raids ensued between them and the whites.

With the establishment of British rule at the Cape, the settlement of about 5000 Britons in the Eastern Cape in 1820, and measures abolishing the vagrancy laws against the Hottentots in 1828 and emancipating the slaves in 1834, a new dimension of conflict was added to the South African scene. All subsequent history must be analyzed in terms of a triangular conflict between the Boers (later known as "Afrikaners") and the British, and between both of these white groups and the African majority. In 1836 the Boers started on their Great Trek and in a sweeping expansion invaded what is today the Province of Natal where they clashed with both the Zulu and the British. The British annexed Natal and most of the Afrikaners withdrew into what soon became the Boer Republics of the Transvaal and the Orange Free State. A series of conflicts between the whites and the African nations (Zulu, Ndebele, Sotho) ended in the elimination of the African nations as independent states and as military forces by 1880.

From that date the English and the Afrikaners ruled supreme over their respective parts of South Africa, and the conflict between the two white groups was intensified; the main economic stakes of the struggle were the control of the Kimberley diamond fields (discovered in 1867) and the Witwatersrand gold deposits (opened in 1886). This contest between Boer expansionism and British imperialism culminated in the second Anglo-Boer War of 1899 to 1902 (a first Anglo-Boer War occurred on a much smaller scale in 1880) which ended in British victory and led in 1910 to the formation of the Union of South Africa as a politically autonomous state under the joint control of local English and Afrikaner settlers. The Africans, the Coloureds, and the Indians (who, beginning in 1860, were introduced by the English from India to work as indentured laborers on the sugar cane plantations of Natal) were not consulted in the settlement between the two white groups and were given virtually no voice in the conduct of the new state's affairs (except for qualified franchise rights in the Cape Province). Only the European languages, English and

Afrikaans (derived from Dutch), were given official standing. The Union (since 1961 Republic) of South Africa was launched on its career as a racist *"Herrenvolk* democracy," that is, as a state in which a white minority of 20 per cent ruled itself democratically but imposed its tyranny over a nonwhite majority of 80 per cent.

Although the political structure of South Africa has remained basically unchanged since 1910, profound economic transformations have made the country by far the most urbanized south of the Sahara and an industrial giant by African standards. The three largest cities in sub-Saharan Africa (Johannesburg, Cape Town, and Durban) are located in South Africa; the economy became increasingly diversified, with manufacturing and services overshadowing both agriculture and mining; between 1912 and 1958 the national income increased over fifteen times [4]. These processes of urbanization and industrialization have been accelerated during World War I and II and have created conditions of intense racial competition as nonwhites became better skilled, educated, and able to take over occupations held by whites, and as "poor whites" were displaced from the land and forced to migrate to cities with few industrial skills.

South Africa is probably the most complex and the most conflict-ridden of the world's multiracial societies [5]. The most salient lines of cleavage are those of race. According to the dominant group's definition of the situation, the population is divided into four rigid color-castes: the Europeans or whites numbering slightly under 20 per cent; the Indians accounting for some 3 per cent; the Coloureds numbering somewhat less than 10 per cent; and the Africans who number 68 per cent of the total (see Table 5.1). The last three groups are collectively referred to as the "non-Europeans" or "nonwhites," and the caste-line between whites and nonwhites is even more impermeable than that between the three nonwhite castes.

Contrary to government claims that these group boundaries are culturally defined, the castes are racially determined. Thus the Coloureds are completely westernized (except for a small group of "Cape Malays" who have remained Muslims); they are Christians, speak Afrikaans or English, and are culturally as indistinguishable from Europeans as Negro Americans are from white Americans. Yet they are regarded as non-Europeans by virtue

RACE AND RACISM

TABLE 5.1

Racial Groups as Percentages of Total South African
Population (1904–1960)

Year	Whites	Africans	Asians	Coloureds	All Non-whites	Total All Races (in thousands)
1904	21.6	67.4	2.4	8.6	78.4	5,176
1911	21.4	67.3	2.5	8.8	78.6	5,973
1921	21.9	67.8	2.4	7.9	78.1	6,929
1936	20.9	68.8	2.3	8.0	79.1	9,590
1946	20.8	68.6	2.5	8.1	79.2	11,418
1951	20.9	67.5	2.9	8.7	79.1	12,648
1960	19.4	68.2	3.0	9.4	80.6	15,982

of their physical characteristics. Similarly, westernized Indians and Africans cannot lose their ascribed caste status. Membership in one of the four castes is by birth and for life. A person's race appears on his identity card and "passing" is technically impossible. However, in the three centuries before the Population Registration Act was introduced in 1950 to prevent "passing," tens if not hundreds of thousands of light Coloureds did enter the white group and a great many Africans passed for Coloured. Today the only caste where membership is not completely hereditary is the Coloured one; offspring of parents of different castes can be classified as Coloured.

Miscegenation is severely condemned by the white group, both in law and in custom, although it continues to take place clandestinely on a small scale. Both intermarriage and "indecent or immoral acts" between whites and nonwhites are forbidden by law and subject to severe penalties (up to seven years in prison). Although intermarriage and sexual relations between the three nonwhite castes are not legally forbidden, they are uncommon, and all four racial groups may be regarded as virtually endogamous [6].

The four castes are clearly in a hierarchy of power, wealth, and prestige. Each race has a legally defined set of privileges or disabilities. Wide differences in standards of living, formal education, health, occupation, and wages accompany the vastly unequal distribution of power. The whites retain a virtual monopoly of both power and wealth. With the exception of a residual and almost meaningless franchise exercised by the Coloureds in the Cape Province on a racially segregated voters' roll, the national electorate is entirely white; the bicameral parliament in Cape Town is all white, and so are the cabinet, the army, the navy, the judiciary, and all the higher positions in the civil service (except for the machinery of puppet chiefs set up by the government in the Native Reserves now being restyled as Bantustans). The few political rights that the nonwhites enjoyed in 1910 were gradually eliminated, and South Africa is in effect a white government with an internal colonial empire in which the Africans (and increasingly the Coloureds and Indians) are dealt with administratively and arbitrarily without any representation on sovereign lawmaking bodies. The whites also monopolized the means of violence: military service and the right to carry firearms are limited to whites. (The police force uses nonwhites, but does not arm them with firearms.)

The political and military power of the Europeans has been translated into, and is further entrenched by, an impressive array of economic privileges. A rural white population of less than half a million owns 87 per cent of the land, whereas nearly four million Africans are squeezed into the remaining 13 per cent which make up the impoverished, eroded, overgrazed Native Reserves. The whites keep for themselves almost all better-paying occupations, including skilled manual work. The nonwhites are left with domestic service, semiskilled and unskilled jobs in industry, mining, and agriculture, some small-scale retail trade and petty white-collar occupations, mostly among Coloureds and Indians, and selected professions such as schoolteaching and nursing for "their own people" in racially segregated institutions. When scarcity of white labor has forced industrialists to employ nonwhites in more skilled jobs, this is done surreptitiously and at greatly discriminatory rates of pay. The principle of unequal pay for equal work has even been applied by most religious denominations in paying widely different stipends for white and African clergymen. The mean family income of whites is approximately thirteen to fourteen times that of Africans and five times that of Coloureds and Indians. Numbering less than 20 per cent of the population, the whites earned 67 per cent of the national income in 1960 [7]. Government educational expenditures per white pupil are ten times those per African pupil. In the towns the whites occupy all the better residential areas and throughout the country they enjoy a lion's share of all the public facilities. Indeed, the Reservation of Separate Amenities Act explicitly legalizes not only segregated facilities but also unequal ones; quite often no amenities at all are provided for nonwhites; thus in a park, for example, all benches are often labeled "Europeans Only."

Among the nonwhite groups the Coloureds suffer the smallest number of disabilities, although they are almost completely excluded from national politics. The Indians, on the average, are somewhat better off economically than the Coloureds, but they have been subjected to a more hostile government policy and to more restrictions than the Coloureds (though fewer than the Africans). Coloureds and Indians occupy an intermediate status between the whites and the Africans, but they are closer to the Africans than to the whites.

The Africans, who by themselves constitute more than two thirds of the population, bear the brunt of political oppression and economic exploitation. Through their labor they create most of the country's wealth, but they receive only one fourth of the national income (26.5 per cent in 1960) [8]. Although they are the poorest group, they pay a disproportionate share of taxes; they have no voting rights except in the puppet Bantustan of the Transkei where the white government can overrule any decision of the local African "representatives" (most of whom are appointed rather than elected). Over a million Africans are arrested and convicted each year—the vast majority of them for purely technical offenses against discriminatory laws or regulations such as the "pass laws" to which only nonwhites are subject. The geographical mobility of Africans, their family life, and their freedom to seek work in the open market are severely limited by "pass laws," "influx control," "job reservation," "group area" laws, and numerous other pieces of apartheid legislation. The entire lifetime of the African is spent under the burden of economic exploitation and the shadow of police surveillance, intimidation, and brutality. In the urban ghettoes where Africans are forced to live, often separated by restrictive laws from their spouses and children, the inmates are free neither to come nor to go and are but one arbitrary step away from prison.

Next in importance to the racial lines of cleavage and their social, economic, and political concomitants are the cultural or ethnic divisions in South Africa. Cultural or ethnic groups overlap only partly with racial groups. Race and culture are thus not only analytically distinct but also empirically so. To the extent that cultural criteria, foremost among which are language and religion, cut across the color castes, existing racial conflicts are further exacerbated. For example, Afrikaans- and English-speaking Coloureds have long aspired to become assimilated with their respective white language group, but they have been denied admission purely on the basis of race.

Politically the most important linguistic cleavage is between English- and Afrikaans-speaking whites who constitute respectively some 40 and 60 per cent of the dominant group. This old conflict has been most overt when the common threat of African opposition was felt to be most securely under control. With the post-World War II emergence among Africans of mass militancy along modern political lines, the tension between the English and the Afrikaners has again receded into the background of South African politics. The slogan is for white unity against the "black peril." However, real conflicts of interest remain between these two white ethnic groups concerning the use of the two national languages in the government and the schools as well as the inequality of occupational and educational status between them. (The English-speaking whites tend to be of higher social class status than the Afrikaners.) In addition, the Afrikaners have since 1948 monopolized political power, whereas the English own the bulk of the country's extractive and manufacturing industries, and control much of banking, finance, and commerce. Religiously, the whites are divided among the Protestants, Catholics, and Jews; the Afrikaners are almost exclusively Protestants belonging to the Dutch Reformed Churches, while the English-speaking whites are religiously divided.

The main language and religious groups represented among whites are also present among nonwhites, since missionary activities and other forms of culture contact spread Christianity, the use of European languages, and Western education. More non-whites than whites speak English and/or Afrikaans, either as their mother tongue or as a second language; similarly, for every white Christian there are approximately two nonwhite Christians. The Coloureds are overwhelmingly Afrikaans-speaking and Protestant; the Indians are mostly Hindus and Muslims and belong to five main Indian language groups, but almost all speak fluent English. The Africans are in majority Christians and speak several related Bantu languages (the major ones being Zulu, Xhosa, and Sotho) as their mother tongues, but most urban men also know either English or Afrikaans, or both.

In spite of government attempts to revive the significance of ethnic distinctions among Africans through a policy of mother-tongue instruction in schools, linguistically based Bantustans, and government-sponsored revivalism and glorification of tradi-tional African culture, language distinctions and ethnic chauvin-ism are rapidly subsiding in importance among urban Africans. What has been misleadingly and invidiously termed "tribalism" is certainly more prevalent among whites than nonwhites. In fact, the very endeavor by the dominant whites to inculcate ethnic particularism among Africans has probably contributed to their drive toward westernization and even deprecation of indigenous African cultures. However, the existence of ethnic heterogeneity among nonwhites has been used by the government not only as a method of dividing and ruling but also as an alibi for racism. Faced with accusations of racial discrimination, the government fallaciously claims that apartheid is simply a policy of cultural pluralism.

In addition to the overlapping but discrete cleavages of race and ethnicity, the South African population is stratified into social classes. More precisely, each racial caste is subdivided according to status criteria which range from traditional ones (such as the Hindu caste system among South Africans of Indian origin) to modern socioeconomic strata based on income, educa-tion, occupation, and life-style. This leads to an extremely complex status system that space limitations prevent me from describing here [9]. Because of the all-encompassing and over-whelming importance of race, however, class distinctions tend to take a distinctly secondary place, or indeed a tertiary one, after both race and ethnicity. Similarity of class position across racial lines has never been a successful basis for political action in South Africa, and even the labor movement has been infected by racism. Not only is there an almost total lack of solidarity between white and nonwhite manual workers, but the prevailing feelings have been ones of bitterness and competition. The white worker is in such a pampered, protected, and privileged position as to make his class status, in the Marxian sense of relationship to the means of production, nearly irrelevant.

The ubiquity of race, the confusion between race and culture by the dominant group, and the latter's insistence that racial consciousness and "purity" are essential to its survival make South Africa a society ridden with conflicts and contradictions. To mention but a few of the more obvious contradictions and sources of strain, a rigidly ascribed division of labor based on race is hardly the most efficient way of running a complex industrial economy; similarly, the government's insistence on the maximum degree of spatial segregation compatible with the supply of African labor to "white" industries entails an enormous waste of resources and productivity; the cost of the repressive apparatus needed to suppress African resentment against apartheid policies mounts yearly (e.g., between 1961 and 1964 the military budget increased from 112 million to 291 million dollars).

Yet, far from being resolved, these conflicts and contradictions have become increasingly acute as the dominant group has become more and more reactionary. The few rights of the nonwhites have been steadily eroded by legislation. Segregation measures became more and more inclusive, rigid, and far-reaching as apartheid relentlessly extended from residential areas, primary and secondary schools, means of transport, waiting rooms, hospitals, cemeteries, toilets, and sport facilities to universities, private associations, and religious worship. Interracial contact on a basis other than between master and servant became increasingly penalized by methods ranging from ostracism to imprisonment. The desirability of apartheid and the inability of members of different races to live peacefully together became the official credo, and indeed the very process of enforcing racial segregation made intergroup conflict a self-fulfilling prophecy.

Mutual fear and hostility climbed; discourtesy, violence, and brutality, both public and private, mounted; such tenuous non-utilitarian ties as existed between whites and nonwhites snapped under strain; the possibility of nondiscriminatory behavior, even for the few unprejudiced whites, disappeared; political opinions polarized; white racism called forth black racism; the use of terrorism by the police turned the nonwhite opposition away from Gandhian techniques of passive resistance and toward sabotage; the state steadily improved its machinery of oppression, invested in military hardware, and passed more and more dictatorial legislation which destroyed the rule of law even for the white minority. Having engaged itself on the road to tryranny, the dominant minority soon reached the point of no return where any liberalization of policy might indeed open the floodgates of revolution and result in the extermination or expulsion of the ruling class. The white minority, to use a cliché, maneuvered itself into the position of sitting on top of a self-created volcano of racial hatred with no other place to go. And it seeks its survival in what will probably bring about its demise—its monomaniacal racist compulsion.

This process of political repression can be analyzed in terms of two principal components. The first consists of the apartheid program itself, that is, those pieces of legislation (such as the Group Areas Act, the Bantu Education Act, the Population Registration Act, the Prohibition of Mixed Marriages Act, and many others) specifically aimed at bringing about maximum racial segregation while trying to minimize economic cost and disruption for the dominant white group. This apartheid program has ranged from "macro-segregation" into monoracial regions (the "Bantustans"), to "meso-segregation" into ghettoes within urban areas to "micro-segregation" in the form of separate facilities in situations where close physical proximity is unavoidable, for example, on the job. This first aspect of government policy is part of a systematic, premeditated plan that has been meticulously perfected since the Afrikaner Nationalists came into office in 1948.

The second facet of Nationalist policies concerns the enforcement of this apartheid program. As the program generated increasing hostility among the nonwhites and mounting costs for the dominant Europeans, the government has passed a series of laws effectively abolishing the rule of law for *all* people, including the whites. Such laws as the Suppression of Communism Act, the Public Safety Act, and the Criminal Law Amendment Act have been paradoxically nonracial in character, being also aimed at the few but annoying white radicals. Thus South Africa is in the process of resolving the basic duality of its traditional polity, namely as a democracy for the *Herrenvolk* and a colonial regime for the nonwhites. Tyranny is increasingly extending to the Europeans who are, by and large, willing to pay the price of freedom for their economic and social privileges.

South Africa has often been described as a Fascist state. This characterization shows little understanding of the situation. South Africa is racist but not Fascist. To be sure, some of the police methods and of the legislation used to suppress opposition give the country a superficial similarity with Fascist states. South Africa, however, clearly lacks most crucial elements of Fascism, notably the presence of a charismatic leader, a high degree of militarism, the endeavor to create a monolithic nation and to include all institutions within a single political party, and intensive propaganda in a collectivist ideology. Apartheid, on the other hand, aims to compartmentalize the country and to perpetuate distinct racial and ethnic groups. A much closer parallel to South Africa than Nazi Germany or Fascist Italy is the southern part of the United States at the height of Jim Crow.

Apartheid, in my opinion, ought to be interpreted as an endeavor to reestablish the old paternalistic master-servant relations that prevailed in the pastoral Boer Republics of the nineteenth century [10]. At the ideological level apartheid is a romantic leap into a half-mythical past when the Africans "knew their place," when the evils of urbanization had not yet corrupted them and made them "cheeky," when missionaries, liberals, and "outside agitators" had not yet meddled in South Africa's affairs, when the "Bantu" were simple but noble savages, and when white supremacy was unquestioned.

This formulation is, of course, oversimplified, and apartheid consists of quite an elaborate set of rationalizations, but apartheid is a living political dinosaur. It is basically an old-fashioned colonial regime coerced through the dynamics of industrialization into modernizing its repressive apparatus. Apartheid aims at reversing the westernization of Africans by using mother-tongue instruction in schools; preventing as many nonwhites as possible from settling in the "white" cities; tolerating Africans in cities only insofar as they provide menial labor for the whites; achieving the minimum amount of equalitarian contact between racial groups and the maximum amount of segregation consistent with economic development; and recreating a series of pseudo-traditional Bantustans established along ethnic lines, and ruled paternalistically through a system of indirect rule. This reactionary utopia would not have much chance of success even in the more agrarian countries to the north of the Limpopo. In a highly industrialized and urbanized country like South Africa, the preservation of a rigidly ascribed system of racial castes, of a series of ethnic groups living in cultural isolation, and of a minority white settler regime is doomed to failure.

In the process of trying to implement their blueprint the Afrikaner Nationalist government has faced growing opposition and has resorted to an increasingly naked use of coercion. Whatever condescending and supercilious benevolence toward the "Bantu" may have motivated the early architects of apartheid, and may still delude its academic proponents, has degenerated into an increasingly ruthless and efficient police state. In the words of Hilda Kuper in a recent book review, "South Africa has become a vast and terrifying prison." Consensus is almost totally absent, and South Africa is held together in a condition of "static disequilibrium" through a grim mixture of political coercion and economic interdependence. However exploited the Africans are, they depend for sheer physical survival on wage employment in the money economy. To withdraw one's labor is to face nearly immediate starvation. The price of survival at the minimum subsistence level is exploitation, oppression, and degradation. But three million people cannot indefinitely repress the frustration and fury of thirteen million people who live in their midst. A South Africa divided against itself awaits its impending doom.

NOTES

[1] The bibliography lists a few of the more important works on South Africa. A much more extensive bibliography and treatment of many of the ideas

contained in this chapter can be found in my *South Africa, A Study in Conflict.* Also particularly germane are Leo Kuper's *An African Bourgeoisie;* Leo Marquard's *The Peoples and Policies of South Africa;* C. W. De Kiewiet's *A History of South Africa, Social and Economic;* and Sheila Patterson's *Colour and Culture in South Africa.*

[2] In addition to numerous travelogues, diaries, and other eye-witness accounts that give a vivid picture of slavery at the Cape, the best secondary sources on South African slavery are C. G. Botha, *Social Life in the Cape Colony in the 18th Century;* Isobel E. Edwards, *Towards Emancipation;* and J. S. Marais, *The Cape Colored People.*

[3] Marais, *loc. cit.*

[4] van den Berghe, *op. cit.,* pp. 89–90.

[5] For more detailed accounts of contemporary South Africa see van den Berghe, *loc. cit.;* Leo Marquard, *loc. cit.;* and Sheila Patterson, *loc. cit.*

[6] In 1946, before the passage of the Prohibition of Mixed Marriages Act, only one white out of 714 married outside his "race." The respective figures for Coloureds, Indians and Africans were one in 20, one in 31, and one in 67. Cf. Pierre L. van den Berghe. "Miscegenation in South Africa," p. 72.

[7] van den Berghe, *op. cit.,* p. 303.

[8] *Ibid.*

[9] More extensive accounts can be found in Leo Kuper's *An African Bourgeoisie,* and in my own two books, *South Africa* and *Caneville.* Hilda Kuper's *Indian People in Natal* gives a more detailed view of the Indian group.

[10] The polemical and scholarly literature is abundant. For factual information and for interpretations differing from my own, see Gwendolen Carter, *The Politics of Inequality;* Sheila Patterson, *The Last Trek;* Jordan Ngubane, *An African Explains Apartheid;* Muriel Horrell, *A Survey of Race Relations in South Africa;* Albert Luthuli, *Let My People Go;* and N. J. Rhoodie and H. J. Venter, *Apartheid.*

VI

An Analytical Comparison

We have just completed a cursory survey of a vast amount of data about four large-scale and complex societies. These data, however, have not been presented in a directly comparable form. To have achieved this aim would have meant cutting up the presentation of the case studies into a series of analytical categories. This would not only have grievously interfered with whatever readability this book may have, but it would also have destroyed any possibility of treating each society as a relatively autonomous whole, profoundly altered over time as a consequence of the complex interplay between its constituent elements. I have therefore adopted a holistic, historical treatment of the four case studies and only loosely imposed on my factual presentation the analytical constraint of my comparative typology. In an endeavor to arrive at a more systematic comparison I shall follow a two-step procedure. First, I shall present a brief synopsis of essential aspects in which the four case studies resemble or differ from one another. Second, I shall attempt to derive some meaningful generalizations about our material at a higher level of abstraction.

Similarities and Differences

1. **Conquest.** All four societies are the products of a historically unique set of factors which resulted in the colonial expansion

of Europe since the late fifteenth century. Military conquest is commonly the origin of plural societies, but this was a rather special form of conquest: it involved the maritime expansion of a few people with a superior military and naval technology. The actual form of the conquest differed, although in all cases it involved extensive conflict between the native and the invading populations. In Mexico Cortés conducted a *Blitzkrieg* which subjected most of the population to direct Spanish rule within a few years. In the other three societies European expansion was more gradual; it involved a protracted series of frontier skirmishes with a number of indigenous groups and lasted through most of the nineteenth century.

Through their common historical roots, these four societies are not entirely independent of one another. Although they had little direct contact with each other until the twentieth century (except for Mexico and the United States where massive contact began, inauspiciously, in the mid-nineteenth century), all four countries were parts of far-reaching colonial empires of culturally related European powers. Consequently, there was a measure of global politico-economic integration and conflict between them. The New World was heavily involved in Africa through the slave trade, and the colonial powers clashed extensively with one another over the control of both the slave trade and the colonies.

2. *Cultural and Social Pluralism.* Pluralism characterizes all four societies, through not to the same degree nor in the same way. Cultural pluralism (as indexed both by the amount of cultural difference between ethnic groups living within the same society and by the relative size and power of these groups) ranges from minimal in the United States to maximal in South Africa, with Mexico and Brazil in an intermediate position.

In the United States the overwhelming majority of the population (i.e., all except recent immigrants and a scattering of Indian and Eskimo groups) has become acculturated to the dominant New World version of European culture. African cultures have been virtually obliterated among slaves; whatever small cultural differences exist between Negroes and whites (after controlling for social class) are the products more of cultural "drift" as a result of segregation than of surviving African traits. American Indians have either become encapsulated in numerically and socially insignificant enclaves or culturally assimilated to surrounding white, Negro, or Mexican-American communities. Most immigrant groups have become assimilated within two or three generations of their arrival, with, however, differential rates of acculturation for Northern Europeans, Southern and Eastern Europeans, Spanish Americans, and Asians. Secondary cultural pluralism in the form of age, class, religious and regional subcultures and of residual ethnic traits (such as cooking), does, of course, exist in the United States, but major cultural cleavages are absent.

At the other extreme, cultural pluralism in South Africa is a prominent aspect of the society. Each of the five major languages (Afrikaans, Xhosa, Zulu, Sotho, and English) are spoken by two to three million people; four major cultural traditions are represented (southeastern Bantu, Hindu, Islamic, and the Western European Judeo-Christian), with each subdivided into several language groups. Although there has been a general tendency for Western culture to gain ground at the expense of the others, the process is still far from complete. Furthermore, countervailing forces may even reverse the process, unlikely though this prospect seems at present.

Mexico and Brazil occupy intermediate positions on the scale of cultural pluralism. Iberian culture clearly dominates in both of these countries. The New World versions of Spanish and Portuguese cultures, however, have been more influenced by indigenous elements, and in Brazil by African elements than their English counterpart in the United States. Furthermore, in Mexico and, to a more limited extent, in Brazil the culturally non-western minorities remain proportionately more important than in the United States.

With respect to social pluralism (i.e., the institutional segmentation of the social structure as distinct from cultural differences) the picture is different. South Africa, with its rigid system of color castes and its deliberate policy of institutional segregation and quadruplication, leads the way in structural as well as cultural pluralism. To complicate matters further the cultural lines of cleavage overlap only in part with the social ones. In terms of social pluralism the United States would come second with its Negro-white division, which is an almost pure case of social as distinguished from cultural pluralism. Brazil shows the development of some parallel institutional structures between Afro- and Euro-Brazilians, though not to the same extent as in the United States. Mexico, though somewhat more culturally pluralistic than Brazil, is probably less socially pluralistic insofar as the Catholic Church has imposed on both Indians and mestizos a common institutional framework that transcends cultural differences.

3. Dominant Religion. Religious differences between Protestantism and Catholicism have been stressed by many authors as among the most important factors causing differences in systems of race relations [1]. We shall return to that point later. However, beyond the similarities between Spain and Portugal as Catholic powers and England and Holland as Protestant nations, there were important differences in the role of the Church in Brazil and in Mexico. In Mexico the Church was at once the religious branch of the Spanish colonial establishment and a major political and economic power in its own right. Mexican prelates were powerful by virtue of their position in the Church, but they were also rich aristocrats through their social origin. In Brazil the Church never enjoyed such political and economic parity with the state and the lay aristocracy. Its interests were subordinate of those of the lay settlers and indeed often clashed with them.

4. Indigenous Level of Social Organization. In Mexico the Spaniards encountered large centralized states, confederated into complex empires, with considerable social stratification, urbanization, intensive agriculture, and relatively dense settlement. In the United States and Brazil the Europeans clashed primarily with nomadic or seminomadic groups that were not urbanized and showed only incipient political centralization and social stratification. In South Africa the Boers first met nomadic pastoralists and hunters but later had to contend with medium-sized agricultural nation-states without urbanization but with some degree of stratification and a high amount of political centralization and military organization. On this dimension South Africa thus falls in between Mexico on the one hand and Brazil and the United States on the other.

5. *Fate of the Indigenous Population.* In the United States the indigenous population was nearly exterminated and its remnants were relegated to "reservations." Much the same happened in Brazil, but, in addition, significant numbers mixed genetically with the Europeans, adopted Portuguese culture, and became assimilated to the dominant group. In Mexico there was first a drastic reduction of the Indian population as a result mostly of epidemics and forced labor, but thereafter the indigenous people miscegenated with Spaniards and Africans and became hispanicized, except in some remote "refuge areas" where Indian communities survive to the present. In South Africa the Bushmen were wiped out or pushed back to the Kalahari Desert, the Hottentots intermixed with the Boers and became westernized, and the Bantu-speaking groups were politically subjected but retained to a considerable extent their cultural and genetic identity.

6. *Miscegenation.* Extensive biological intermixture existed in all four societies, particularly in the period prior to the twentieth century. Thereafter miscegenation probably declined in the United States, Brazil, and South Africa. In Brazil and Mexico there was extensive intermixture with both Indians and African slaves. In the United States whites mixed with Negroes to a much greater extent than with either Indians or other nonwhite immigrant groups, but after the abolition of slavery, there was probably a sharp decline in miscegenation [2]. In South Africa interracial mixture took place mostly in the Cape between Boers, Hottentots, and slaves; there was a decline in the frequency of miscegenation after the Great Trek, as witnessed by the relatively small number of Coloureds in the Transvaal, the Orange Free State, and Natal.

7. *Extent of Slavery.* Until the second half of the nineteenth century the economies of Brazil and the United States were dependent on slave labor to a much greater extent than those of South Africa and Mexico. In Mexico Indian peonage made slavery unprofitable and obsolete by the eighteenth century. In South Africa only the Western Cape (i.e., the area around Cape Town) relied heavily on imported slave labor; elsewhere the reduction of Hottentots and black Africans to serfdom and later migrant contract labor and Indian indenture were resorted to as sources of semi-voluntary toil. In both Brazil and the United States slave trading and slave labor were the direct or indirect bases of a substantial proportion of the money economy until 1888 and 1865 respectively. In all four cases the labor of the subordinate groups could until recent decades be described as unfree, whether serfdom, indenture, debt peonage, or chattel slavery prevailed.

8. *Demographic Variables.* In terms of racial composition, immigration, internal migration, and regional concentration by race, the four countries vary substantially. Brazil and the United States have a number of demographic characteristics and trends in common: both countries increased their population greatly by large-scale immigration from overseas; until the mid-nineteenth century immigration was mostly involuntary and from Africa; thereafter it became voluntary and was mostly of European and secondarily of Asian origin. The pattern of regional concentration and internal migration by race was also similar in Brazil and the United States. In both countries the Negro population was heavily concentrated in a major region (the Northeast in Brazil, the Southeast in the United States), and starting in the late nineteenth century there was a progressive dispersion of the Negro population to other regions. When we examine racial distribution macroscopically, we note an increasing spacial homogenization by race, although in the United States and to some extent in Brazil this *regional dispersion* was accompanied by *local concentration* by race in urban working-class slums. Both Brazil and the United States are predominantly "white" according to the respective social definitions of that term, even though this was not true for Brazil prior to the twentieth century.

South Africa and Mexico differ from Brazil and the United States in terms of most demographic aspects of race relations. In both South Africa and Mexico the whites have always been in minority. Transoceanic immigration into Mexico and South Africa from Africa, Asia, and Europe took place, but not on a massive enough scale to upset greatly the "racial" composition of the country. In terms of international but *intracontinental* migration South Africa is the recipient and Mexico the exporter of much transient labor. In Mexico, except for the concentration of Negroes in the coastal areas and the capital during colonial times, there have been no major regional concentrations of people of different racial groups. In South Africa there has been a moderate degree of geographical concentration by race in that Indians are concentrated in coastal Natal, Coloureds in the Western Cape, and Africans in rural areas; but both whites and nonwhites are found almost everywhere, and the whites are in minority in nearly all rural and urban areas.

9. *Economic basis.* All four countries underwent a process of economic diversification characterized by a growth in the complexity of the division of labor and in the relative importance of the secondary and tertiary sectors (manufacturing and services). Industrialization has proceeded furthest in the United States, with South Africa in second place (if one includes extractive industries). Originally, all four economies were based predominantly on agriculture and mining, but Brazil and the United States had a less diversified agriculture than the other two countries. Latifundiary monoculture did not characterize Mexico and South Africa to the same extent as it did Brazil and the United States, but reliance on mining (of silver in Mexico, gold and diamonds in South Africa) was conversely greater. Much of the agricultural production of Brazil and the United States, and indeed the overwhelming bulk of the slave-grown production in these countries, was a commercial undertaking for export, whereas Mexican and South African agriculture was mostly for domestic consumption.

10. *Major Lines of Cleavage and Dimensions of Conflict.* In the long history of violent conflict in South Africa the main cleavages have been almost always on either racial or ethnic lines. Since the early nineteenth century English and Afrikaners have opposed one another in a long sequence of incidents culminating in the Second Anglo-Boer War of 1899-1902; whites and the various indigenous groups have confronted each other in a series of frontier wars from the seventeenth to the nineteenth century and more recently in a bitter political struggle. In United States history race and ethnicity have also been important, although not the sole, dimensions of conflict. Frontier wars with Indians and the long dispute over the extension of slavery which led to the Civil War dominated the nineteenth century. International affairs on issues such as relations with Japan over immigration and the history of United States imperialism and expansionism in the Western Hemisphere have been influenced directly by racism. Even today the salience of race in internal conflicts and group violence is obvious, and it is not difficult to find evidence of racism in the conduct of American foreign policy.

The situations in Mexico and Brazil are clearly different from those in South Africa and the United States. In the Latin American countries the ethnic and racial aspects of conflict subsided in importance after the period of conquest. By the time of Independence in Mexico social class and political factionalism had become the major dimensions of internal conflict. The Revolution had, of course, some ethnic undertones reflected in an ideology of *indigenismo,* but it was fought predominantly on social and political issues like land distribution and presidential succession. Brazil enjoyed, by and large, a less turbulent history than the other three countries, but, as in Mexico, the relative salience of race and ethnicity in conflicts has been low. Regionalism, political factionalism (such as the traditional army-navy rivalry), and more recently social class have defined the major lines of cleavage in Brazil. In colonial times the conflict between the Jesuits and the lay settlers, though it revolved around the treatment of Indians, was not directly ethnic or racial.

11. *Attitudes and Policies of the Dominant Group.* All four societies have a colonial past with a history of autocratic rule over, and economic exploitation of, the indigenous or slave population. However, South Africa and the United States have been characterized by a much more overt and virulent form of racism and by a system of rigid color castes. Colonial Mexico also had a fairly rigid structure of *castas* partially based on race, but these distinctions became obsolete early in the nineteenth century. Although Brazil never had a system of *castas* like that of New Spain, concern over race has survived longer than in Mexico and racial prejudice is still very much alive, though in more subdued form than in the United States and South Africa.

Political ideology and attitudes toward cultural and social assimilation are related to racial attitudes. South African whites have not only been intensely racist but they have also been extremely conservative or even reactionary in their general political ideology; and they have (except for some missionary groups and for some liberal intellectuals) been opposed to both the cultural and the social assimilation of the non-Europeans. Apartheid is a blueprint for the tight compartmentalization of South Africa into racial and ethnic pigeonholes. At the other extreme, Mexico with its militant anti-racist ideology has also undergone a radically anticlerical and socialist revolution and has favored the cultural, racial, and social assimilation of Indian minorities into the national culture. Although the political past of Brazil has been marked by shifts between the right and the left, the dominant ideology has been both anti-racist and assimilationist as in Mexico. In the United States, on the other hand, the dominant group and the Federal government have supported racial segregation and discrimination until World War II, and the local and state governments still do in the South. This racism has been accompanied by general social conservatism and by attitudes favorable to cultural assimilation (particularly of white immigrants) but hostile to the social assimilation of the nonwhite groups into the national structure, except in a subordinate capacity.

Some Generalizations

Having listed some of the more important similarities and differences between the four multiracial societies studied in previous chapters, can we now go one step further and do what to many historians is an anathema and to most sociologists their *raison d'être*—to generalize?

To be sure, few absolutes or universals are found in all human societies, and each society or culture is in some respects unique. But this is not to say that meaningful generalizations are impossible. Indeed, the aim of comparative sociology is to determine the social, spacial, and temporal boundaries within which generalizations are valid. The alternative—the endless accumulation of descriptive, monographic studies or of masses of statistical data as an end in itself—can hardly be satisfying to any but the most atheoretical of historians and hyper-empiricists.

Before turning to the task of generalizing about race relations, let us briefly characterize the classical distinction between "historicism" and "scientism", and try to show how the seeming contradictions between the two positions rest, in fact, on a false antinomy. On the one hand, extreme historicism insists on the uniqueness of each society and epoch, and concludes that the social sciences cannot transcend description, at least not when they endeavor to deal holistically with complex and large-scale social systems. (A slightly less extreme form of historicism consists of maintaining that, although there are some uniformities, the latter concern superficial or trivial elements of social reality, and that the fundamental eludes generalization because it is unique, i.e., time- and space-specific.) On the other hand, the scientistic position holds that social behavior is repeated, normative, and predictable, and that social scientists should be concerned with developing a universally applicable theory of human behavior. (Again, a more moderate version of scientism allows for non-repeated idiosyncracies of detail, but still maintains that in all its essentials social reality can potentially be explained and predicted in terms of general theory.)

Like most controversies of this nature this one is based on a false antinomy. This is true in two different ways. First, given any empirical reality, some of its elements will be common to all phenomena of the same nature, some of its elements will be common to only some otherwise similar phenomena, and some will indeed be quite idiosyncratic. This is the principle underlying scientific taxonomies. Second, any generalization applies only to a specific universe of phenomena (even if that universe is *the* Universe) under specific conditions. Science ultimately deals both with the manifold manifestations of the unique and the idiosyncratic aspects of the universal. Notwithstanding the etymology, we forget that the unique and the universal are but two facets of the same thing. Indeed, at the limit, even the universe is unique, but uniqueness is the product of a large number of repeated, normative, and predictable elements. Vice versa, statistical regularities are the result of a multiplicity of diverse and unique phenomena.

Applying this conception, let us try to generalize about race relations, defining our universe as consisting of the four case studies examined earlier. These generalizations might then serve as hypotheses for the larger universe including all multiracial societies that grew out of the expansion of Europe since the late fifteenth century and indeed all other racially pluralistic societies.

1. The system of race relations developed in the premodern phase of the four societies examined showed great similarities despite great differences in the cultures of both dominant and subordinate groups. In all instances a typically paternalistic system united in symbiotic interdependence a servile or quasi-servile labor force (whether indigenous, imported, or both) and a land- and/or slave-owning aristocracy who lived on small, autonomous agrarian settlements and engaged in cash agriculture or herding. Close physical proximity between master and slaves (or serfs) was accompanied by great social distance symbolized through caste etiquette, sumptuary regulations, and wide racial disparities in living standards, political power, and legal rights.

The stereotypes of the subordinate groups were similar in that these groups were regarded by the dominant group as inferior, simple, childish, and irresponsible, but acceptable if they stayed in their place. The interracial role structure was based on particularism, ascription, affectivity, and diffuseness (to use Parsons' pattern variables); asymmetry and complementarity of roles along racial lines were stressed according to a model which resembled that between parent and child in the nuclear family. The dominant group rationalized its position by virtue of cultural and racial superiority, often failing to distinguish clearly between race and culture.

These broad similarities in systems of race relations indicate that, given the establishment of political control by a group that differs both culturally and physically from the conquered or subject groups and given a preindustrial system of production, there results a fairly stable type of caste society with well-defined characteristics. These similarities are basic enough to determine within fairly specific limits the stratification system, the interracial role structure, the nature of the polity, and the relations of production.

2. These paternalistic regimes were all characterized by two social processes that profoundly influenced their development. First, a process of physical intermixture or miscegenation took place, almost exclusively through the institutionalization of asymmetrical concubinage between men of the dominant group and women of the subordinate group or groups. Whatever attitudes against miscegenation later developed in the United States and South Africa did not exist during the slavery period. Interracial concubinage, being the sexual expression of a more general pattern of exploitation, flourished under all regimes of chattel slavery as well as under the *encomienda* or *hacienda* system. Far from being an index of "liberalism," the presence of asymmetrical miscegenation under conditions of servitude is a measure of the helpless subordination of the slave or serf women. Miscegenation was, of course, also a consequence of close physical propinquity and constant interaction between masters and servants. In addition, the bearing of mulatto or mestizo offspring brought with it the possibility of improved status for the slave mother and her children and of pecuniary and other advantages to the master. Although miscegenation was more blatantly a form of sexual athleticism and patriarchal harem-keeping in the Iberian colonies (where it became an expression of virility or *machismo*), it was probably equally widespread in the United States and the Cape Colony in South Africa.

Second, paternalistic regimes were accompanied by extensive and relatively rapid assimilation of the subject groups to the culture of the dominant group. This acculturation process was not so much a function of demographic ratios, for it was not significantly impeded by the small proportion of Europeans in Mexico and Brazil; nor did westernization result simply from a deliberate policy of the dominant group. The process does not seem to have been appreciably slower in the United States and the Cape Province of South Africa prior to the nineteenth century where the dominant group did little to encourage it or even tried to prevent it as compared to Mexico and Brazil where the colonists often fostered it at the point of the sword [3].

Rather, the rapidity and thoroughness of westernization appear to have been a function of the brutality with which the subordinate groups have been "deculturated" first and then reduced to close symbiotic subservience. In Mexico, the Spaniards did their best to destroy indigenous cultures and impose Christianity; however, their success was neither immediate nor complete because, although they effectively "decapitated" the Indian civilizations, they did not succeed in atomizing the local peasant community. Chattel slavery as practiced in Brazil, the United States, and the Cape Province was of unrivaled efficiency in stripping slaves of their native culture, because it utterly dehumanized the slave and destroyed even his smallest social unit, the nuclear family. When the nuclear family was allowed partially to survive as in Brazil, some aspects of African cultures subsisted and entered the new nation's heritage, but in the United States where slavery was at its most ruthless the obliteration of African cultures was nearly complete. Having been forcibly deculturated, often within one generation, the conquered or enslaved groups had no option but to adopt the culture of their masters with whom they lived in close proximity.

3. Beyond these similarities, there are, of course, important differences between the four case studies. But these differences, far from reducing one to a historicist position, yield lower order generalizations. One of these concerns the contrasting role of Catholicism and Protestantism. Catholicism quickly adopted an actively proselytizing policy among the indigenous or slave population, tolerating no competing faiths but holding to a universalistic conception of the spiritual equality of man. Catholicism did not hesitate to use force to achieve conversion, but it also resorted to cultural syncretism, using indigenous languages and other symbolic forms or vehicles for transmitting the faith. The fundamental assumption was that each human being had a salvageable soul and that, once he had been made to see the light, social conditions had to make it possible for him to achieve salvation. This was the basis of the Church opposition to slavery, of its insistence on the baptism and marriage of slaves and of its attempts to restrict the power of slaveowners.

Protestantism, on the other hand (or at least those branches of it which were dominant in South Africa and the United

States) took an exclusivistic, elitist view of salvation, did not proselytize extensively and tended to regard the true faith as an upper caste privilege. Most dominant denominations sought Biblical rationalizations for slavery, encouraged neither baptism nor marriage of slaves, and remained largely indifferent to the latter's spiritual and temporal welfare.

4. Another "generalizable difference" between the four cases concerns the nature of the indigenous cultures which the conquerors encountered. When the native populations consisted of small, sparsely settled, politically acephalous, nomadic groups (as was true in Brazil, the United States, and the Western Cape in South Africa), the pattern of contact was frontier expansion of the whites (or westernized half-castes) punctuated by sporadic skirmishes, raids, and guerilla warfare. Nomadic hunters or pastoralists, being unused to steady agricultural labor and being easily decimated by epidemic diseases, were of limited use as slaves or serfs as shown by abortive attempts at Indian slavery by the Portuguese in Brazil. Only the frontier Boers who were themselves semi-nomadic pastoralists found the cattle-herding Hottentots of some use as serfs. The general outcome was virtual genocide of the natives, encapsulation of their scattered remnants in human game reserves, and the large-scale importation of slave labor mostly from the agricultural societies of Africa.

When, on the other hand, the European conquerors encountered large, densely settled, politically centralized, agricultural, and even urban nation-states (as in Mexico and in parts of South Africa after the 1770s), the outcome was quite different. Military conquest was not accompanied by extermination but by subjugation. The dominant group established its control either by "beheading" the indigenous societies and substituting itself as a new aristocracy, or by using the ruling class of the defeated peoples and ruling through it. In both situations the native masses became politically subordinate and economically exploited through some form of serfdom, forced or "contract" labor, debt peonage, or share-cropping tenancy. The availability of an indigenous helotry obviously reduced the importation of slave or indentured labor. Although some of it occurred in both Mexico and South Africa, in neither case did it take the same relative or absolute proportions as in Brazil or the United States.

5. In all four cases the paternalistic system of race and ethnic relations was undermined by a series of changes in the social infrastructure. In the political sphere aristocratic, colonial, or white settler regimes became transformed into "representative" governments with wider participation in the polity, though in South Africa and until recently in the United States the democratic process was still restricted to the dominant racial caste. However, even these *Herrenvolk* democracies are clearly different from the colonial government or the planter slave-owning oligarchy which preceded them, if only because they were legitimized in terms of an ideology that could be effectively used to challenge the racial *status quo*. Thus these *Herrenvolk* democracies contained the ideological seeds of their own destruction, providing the educated elite within the oppressed groups and the progressive minority of the dominant group with a set of values to deny legitimacy to the established order. (This notion is, of course, related to Myrdal's thesis of the American Dilemma; but unlike Myrdal who places the focus of this ideological contradiction within the dominant group, I believe that this ideological dialectic has operated primarily *between* the conflicting racial groups.)

Economic and demographic transformations were also crucial in breaking down paternalism. With an increasingly complex division of labor, a rising level of industrial and educational skills necessary for adequate job performance, a more and more intricate pattern of functional interdependence between sectors of the economy, and rapid shifts in demand for labor in response to technological changes or general development, the old agrarian pattern of a servile or quasi-servile, lowly skilled, spatially and socially immobile labor force where statuses and roles are rigidly ascribed by race became patently inadequate. Close, diffuse, stable, ascriptive relations were replaced by impersonal, segmental, ephemeral ones. Labor mobility increased in response to industrial demands, and the division of labor along caste lines began to give way to one related to achievement and skill. The particularistic master-servant or patron-client relationship was supplanted by a more universalistic competition for scarce resources.

These economic changes inherent in industrialization had their demographic concomitants in migration and urbanization. The small rural primary group of the plantation was replaced by the mass urban society. The slave or peasant became a proletarian. Hitherto isolated people interacted and became exposed to more efficacious means of protest. Political atomization and internationalization of subservience were replaced by group consciousness and alienation from the dominant group.

Beyond these broad similarities, interesting and indeed enlightening differences appear between the four countries. In Mexico racial distinctions and the *casta* system had become obsolete long before the country entered the industrial era and, consequently, Mexico never developed a competitive system of race relations. It went directly from a paternalistic system of ethno-racial *castas* to a system that was equalitarian with respect to race though not to class. Even in the "refuge areas," where ethnic diversity between Indians and the mestizos remains pronounced and the old paternalistic relationship still persists, as Indians become hispanicized they "pass" into the dominant group. Because the distinction between groups is almost entirely cultural, the processes of industrialization, urbanization, democratization, and mass education slowly erode the ethnic line in a way that is not possible when the social definition of groups stresses racial traits.

This, of course, is a crucial distinction between a system of *ethnic* relations and one of *race* relations: Mexico represents a limiting case of race. Of course, the profound political, ideological, demographic, and economic changes in nineteenth and twentieth century Mexico had an impact on social stratification, and conflict and competition were present, but the cleavages were not along racial lines. As the colonial system of ethno-racial estates broke down, a new system of social classes arose which became increasingly differentiated from race and ethnicity. The Mexican Revolution was first and foremost a *class* conflict.

In the other three societies race continued to be a socially significant aspect of social stratification and, consequently, there was a clear transition from a paternalistic to a competitive system of race relations. Racial conflict and competition became more overt, for the white and nonwhite proletariat and peasantry were no longer shielded from *direct* contact in employment by the servile status of the nonwhites. New mechanisms to insure continued white supremacy were instituted, notably racial segregation and discrimination, which replaced serfdom or slavery with its institutionalized social distance. Segregation sought to minimize potentially equal contact between racial groups; it almost invariably did not apply to situations where status inequality was unequivocal. Deliberate (and often legal) discrimination based on race became an added "safety device" to insure racial inequality of performance or achievement.

As members of the subordinate groups were increasingly urbanized, organized, skilled, and educated, the level of protest and dissatisfaction increased. More and more people, particularly the educated elite of the subordinate groups, came openly to challenge the "place" assigned to them by the dominant group and to question the legitimacy of the entire system. Terrorism and rioting developed on both sides. Stereotypes of the subordinate group changed from the humble, happy-go-lucky, "good" Negro or "Native" who "knew his place" to the cheeky, uppity, insolent, treacherous, sly, violent "new Negro" or "detribalized scum" who threatens the status quo.

Of the three countries where race relations became competitive, Brazil represents by far the mildest example. The level of race prejudice and the salience of race *vis à vis* other criteria of stratification are relatively low. Furthermore, although Brazilians are very conscious of phenotypical differences, there are no clear-cut corporate racial groups; one can speak only of ill-defined and not mutually exclusive categories of like-looking people rather than of corporate groups with rather sharply drawn boundaries as in the United States or South Africa. To complicate matters further, there is no sharp distinction between race and class, and these two elements of stratification impinge on each other in the sense that their variations are not completely independent.

High levels of racial conflict and competition exist in both the United States and South Africa where the cumulative burden of racial bigotry, segregation, economic exploitation, political oppression and terrorism, and social degradation has segmented the society into mutually antagonistic racial castes. In both countries attempts to preserve this rigidly ascriptive racial distinction in the face of countervailing economic, political, and educational trends have been made at the price of a growing economic and social cost, of an increasing use of coercion, and of climbing unrest. In spite of important demographic and cultural differences between these two countries, the salience of racism made for similar repressive policies with similar consequences.

Only with World War II and its aftermath did the development of South Africa and the United States begin to diverge significantly. In the United States where the dominant racial group was in overwhelming majority nationally and in substantial majority in the South, the vicious circle of prejudice, discrimination, and segregation was gradually reversed. This dramatic turn was, of course, the product of very complex causes. The war itself with its stress on an efficient utilization of manpower and with its concomitant upswing in urbanization, migration and industrialization was an important precipitating factor. However, the war simply accelerated pre-existing trends that were constantly heightening the social and economic costs of racial segregation and discrimination for the society at large and the dominant group in particular. The war not only highlighted the absurdity of racism; it also unleashed throughout the world the forces which led in a few years to the demise of European colonialism and to the organized militancy of oppressed racial groups within countries under white domination.

In the United States the reversal of the vicious circle has paradoxically been accompanied by a temporary rise in racial conflict as a result of the phenomenon known as the "revolution of rising expectations." As progress was made, more and more Negroes and progressive whites realized that change was possible and came first to expect and then to demand change at a more rapid pace than it actually took place. Thus the belated, cautious, and gradual implementation of racial equality led to an escalation of demands for "Freedom Now." In spite of real progress, the discrepancy between the level of achievement and the level of Negro expectation has increased in the last few years, and the level of racial conflict and dissatisfaction has risen.

As more people realize that the pace of social change they demand cannot be achieved by conventional means, radicalization of methods of protest also occurs. Furthermore, there is a growing recognition that the goal of racial equality can be expeditiously reached only at the cost of some measure of coercion and of some loss of individual freedom (conventionally defined to include the freedom to discriminate on racial grounds). Finally, and most basically, race is increasingly recognized as an epiphenomenon, and more people arrive at the conclusion that the roots of "racial" problems go much deeper than individual prejudices and that racial discrimination cannot be permanently and effectively abolished without more fundamental political and economic reforms. Although the pace of change has thus far been too slow to avert a rising level of tension, it is probably increasing sufficiently to forestall a violent revolution.

In South Africa the arch conservative and segregationist government of Smuts was overthrown in 1948 by the even more reactionary Afrikaner Nationalists. Far from reversing the vicious circle, the dominant group and its elected government have gone full steam backward in a race to the nineteenth century. By so doing the dominant group, which constitutes only one fifth of the population, is constantly reducing its chances of survival in southern Africa. Yet it is also clear that the whites, as a privileged minority which monopolized status, power, and wealth, would lose a great deal if their country were to become democratic. In this respect South Africa is quite different from the United States, and it is unrealistic to expect the dominant whites to behave differently from the way they do. They have now gone so far on the road of repression that any reversal of policies would most probably precipitate revolution. The whites are now facing an inescapable dilemma: only ruthless oppression can give them a precarious lease on African soil on terms which most of them regard as acceptable, that is, on preferential terms; but any further oppression lowers their chance of eventual survival as a distinct group, or at least heightens the price they will have to pay for it.

NOTES

[1] Cf., among others, Frank Tannenbaum, *Slave and Citizen;* and Gilberto Freyre, *The Masters and the Slaves.*

[2] This was probably a product of two factors. First, there were fewer inter-racial unions than under slavery and second, those that continued to take place became more clandestine, transitory, or commercialized, hence less likely to result in offspring.

[3] For a more detailed treatment of this point see my article, "Racialism and Assimilation in Africa and the Americas."

VII

Social and Cultural Pluralism

Race and racism, I have argued, are best regarded as special cases, whatever the disciplinary perspective from which they are approached. To the physical anthropologist "race" in the genetic sense is a case of subspeciation in *homo sapiens;* to a social psychologist racism is a special instance of prejudice; for the philosopher racism is a particular body of ideas; the political scientist may regard racism as a special kind of political ideology; to an economist race is one of the "nonrational" factors, influencing, to be sure, economic behavior but falling outside the scope of his discipline; a historian may look at race and racism as by-products of, and rationalizations for, Western slavery and colonial expansion; a cultural anthropologist may regard race and racism as traits in the cultural inventory of a people.

All these perspectives and approaches are perfectly legitimate. As Allport noted, race and its derivative phenomena are empirical data to which all behavioral sciences contribute mutually complementary approaches [1]. Here, however, we are more specifically concerned with interpreting the phenomena of race and racism within a more general body of *sociological* theory, a task to which this last chapter is devoted. As suggested in the introduction, the concept of *pluralism* is of crucial importance [2]. From a sociological perspective racial divisions can be regarded as a special instance of *structural* or *social* pluralism as distinguished from ethnic divisions which are a case of *cultural pluralism*.

The relationship between social and cultural pluralism presents problems directly germane to race relations. Most multiracial societies are also multicultural, or at least have once been so. Societies that have stressed race as a criterion of status and of group membership have typically been characterized by cultural heterogeneity in the early part of their history. In fact, so frequent and close is the empirical overlap between race and culture that, in most racist societies, there is no clear distinction between these two factors in the popular perception of group differences. Insofar as a distinction is made, cultural traits are frequently attributed to racial differences according to a folk theory of biological determinism.

Historically, however, when any priority in the emergence of cultural versus racial distinctions can be discovered, racial distinctions follow the cultural. In both the United States and South Africa the system of racial castes did not crystallize until after several decades of contact between whites and nonwhites. In the first two or three decades of Dutch settlement at the Cape, adoption of Christianity through baptism was accompanied by a large measure of acceptance into the dominant group (e.g., in the few cases of religious intermarriage between white settlers and Hottentot women). In the United States the first Negroes entered Virginia in 1619, but for several decades indenture was common for both whites and Negroes and slavery as a distinct status restricted to Negroes did not emerge until the 1660s [3].

Racial segmentation represents, together with other types of caste divisions (such as the *eta* of Japan or the Hindu caste system), one of the most extreme and rigid forms of social pluralism. At the same time cultural pluralism frequently tends to reduce itself as a result of prolonged contact. It follows that, when two or more groups with originally distinct cultural traditions live side by side and become defined in racial terms, the coincidence between race and culture frequently diminishes over time. Typically, members of subordinate racial groups become culturally assimilated into the dominant group, or both the dominant and the subordinate groups adapt culturally to each other and a new syncretistic culture emerges. But cultural amalgamation or homogenization, although almost invariably accompanied by miscegenation, is not incompatible with the persistence of racial pluralism.

In the two Latin American countries studied miscegenation did indeed blur racial distinctions, almost completely in Mexico, and to the extent of preventing the rise of distinct corporate racial groups in Brazil. The United States represents the extreme opposite: neither extensive miscegenation nor nearly complete cultural assimilation of Negroes has undermined significantly the rigidity of the racial castes. The potential social effect of miscegenation was nullified by the simple device of ascribing lower caste status to the offspring of mixed unions, and the social advantages conferred by cultural assimilation were limited to white immigrants. Thus the United States is characterized by the persistence of a far-reaching social pluralism that pervades much of the country's institutional structure and creates much conflict. At the same time *maximal* cultural pluralism (i.e. coexistence of two or more unrelated traditions) is limited to a minute segment of the native-born population (the less than one per cent who are Indians or Eskimos). Even *minimal* cultural pluralism (i.e. regional, class, caste, occupational, or age subcultures) is limited in scope if we consider the size and population of the country [4].

In South Africa a high degree of social pluralism (exhibited through a rigid system of four main racial castes) exists in conjunction with continued cultural pluralism. However, as a result of considerable westernization, the racial and cultural lines of cleavage no longer coincide. Each of the four racial castes is subdivided into ethnic groups, but some of the ethnic groups have members in more than one racial group. (Whites and Coloureds are culturally alike; a majority of both belongs to the Afrikaner ethnic group, whereas a minority of each group is culturally English.) In addition, many individuals are in a process of gradual westernization, which makes their ethnic classification difficult even though their racial status is unambiguous. This lack of overlap between culture and race in South Africa has been one of the main sources of conflict. As in the United States cultural assimilation of the nonwhites has been accompanied by racial rejection. The Coloureds, who for the most part have long hoped that they would be admitted into the *Herrenvolk,* have been most consistently frustrated in their assimilationist aspirations, much as have Negroes in the United States.

Cultural pluralism between ethnic groups cannot exist without institutional duplication and hence without social pluralism; that is, any form of cultural pluralism has a structural facet which can be treated as social pluralism. But when, in addition to ethnicity, race is introduced as a criterion of group membership, a new dimension is added to social pluralism. Race is not the structural counterpart of ethnic heterogeneity, but is an independent criterion according to which a society is segmented. Since race is a more rigid basis of cleavage than ethnicity, social pluralism can subsist longer and, indeed, even in the nearly total absence of cultural pluralism, whereas the converse is not true.

This asymmetry in the relationship between social and cultural pluralism is of fundamental significance. The asymmetry, however, is not so complete as I have just suggested. There exists a complicating factor of *secondary* cultural pluralism arising from structural pluralism. To the extent that a culturally homogeneous society is segmented into racial castes that are segregated, are trying to minimize contact, and only have highly circumscribed and stereotyped relationships with one another, then cultural "drift" can be expected to give rise to subcultural differences. The United States illustrates this phenomenon. Negro slaves were first deculturated, then acculturated to the dominant Western culture. However, over the years, as a result of the color line, the Negro working class and peasantry have developed a subculture that differs in some respects (dialect, family composition, and values) from the dominant white culture, even if one controls for social class. Rather than ascribing such differences to dubious African survivals as did Herskovits [5], it seems more plausible to explain these differences in terms of subcultural patterns arising from "drift" and socioeconomic position. For example, the working class Negro "matrifocal" family is more parsimoniously accounted for in terms of family disorganization during slavery than in terms of a fanciful hypothesis about the survival of African matrilinearity. The matrifocal family described by Frazier is clearly *not* matrilineal [6].

This kind of secondary cultural pluralism derived from social

pluralism is, however, of a minimal nature, that is, it only gives
rise to subcultural varieties of the same tradition. On the other
hand, the social pluralism (based on race or caste), which often
originates in pre-existing cultural pluralism, can in time lead to a
deeper cleavage than ethnicity, as shown by South Africa. Thus
cultural and social pluralism are not simply two facets of the
same reality.

In this brief discussion of the relationship between cultural and
social pluralism, I have tried to show the relevance of the concept
of pluralism to the study of race and ethnic relations. The basic
problems of the interplay between race and culture, of assimilation, of acculturation, of miscegenation, and many others can
usefully be analyzed by looking at societies as only partially integrated wholes segmented into heterogeneous groups with at least
partly conflicting interests and goals. The "macrosociological"
analysis of total societies (most of which show at least some degree
of pluralism) involves among other things the delineation of
group boundaries and of the resulting factional alignments, the
determination of the extent and forms of pluralism, and the
specification of the bases of social integration and of the spheres
of institutional autonomy.

To refine the concept of pluralism somewhat further, it is
useful to analyze pluralistic societies at four main levels: groups,
institutions, values, and individuals. (These levels cut across the
distinction between social and cultural pluralism.) Pluralism at
the *group level* is a function of the number of corporate groups
existing within a society; their relative size; the rigidity and
clarity of group boundaries; and the degree of cultural and/or
social differences between the groups. Thus a society like South
Africa, where a score of numerically sizable ethnic groups representing four distinct cultural traditions live side by side, and
where the dominant group endeavors to make social and spatial
boundaries between the four color castes as impermeable as possible and attempts to contain each caste within its own rigid
institutional structure, scores high on almost every dimension of
pluralism. A country like Mexico, on the other hand, which does
not have castes, where the non-Spanish-speaking population is
only some 10 per cent of the total, and where the Federal government actively follows a policy of assimilation of cultural

minorities, exhibits a relatively low degree of pluralism. The extent to which conflict prevails between groups and the degree to which one group dominates the others are also important dimensions of the group level of analysis.

Although the term *institution* as used here is simply a shorthand device to refer to certain behavioral uniformities in the interaction between members of groups, we can conveniently analyze societies in terms of their institutional structure without direct reference to the individuals or groups that make up this structure. Such a structure is pluralistic insofar as its constituent institutions are functionally homologous, yet diverse in their form and/or numerous. Thus *institutional pluralism is the opposite of functional differentiation.* For example, a society where educational, political, and economic institutions are differentiated from each other and from kinship is not any more pluralistic than a less complex society where this is not the case. However, a society that has several sets of legal, educational, political, and economic institutions which perform homologous (or at least overlapping) functions for different groups of people within that society is more pluralistic than one in which all members interact within the framework of a single set of functionally specialized institutions. Institutional pluralism would be exemplified by a racially segregated school system, or the coexistence of a monetary and a subsistence economy, or the presence of several sets of religious institutions, or the joint enforcement of several systems of family law based on different descent and inheritance rules.

There is often a close empirical relationship between institutional pluralism and the groups to which the institutions apply, but sometimes discrepancies between the two aspects of pluralism occur. For example, in the ante-bellum southern United States, the economic and social institutions connected with slavery applied only to Negroes, but not all Negroes were slaves. Thus the distinction between these two levels of analysis is essential.

A third level in the analysis of pluralism concerns *values.* This raises the important problem of value consensus as a source of social integration. If a set of shared values is one of the most basic elements that define a culture, then it follows that, in a society composed of several distinct cultural traditions, value consensus cannot be the main source of societal integration, as some functionalists have argued. Cultural pluralism is thus characterized by the coexistence of several value systems that may converge on some points and be congruent or complementary on others, but which are generally characterized by some degree of conflict or incompatibility. For example, a system of family laws and values which permits polygyny may exist side by side with one that enjoins monogamy or celibacy. This was true in many former European colonies in Africa.

Social pluralism is also typically accompanied by lack of complete consensus. Although members of several corporate groups (such as races or classes) may share a common culture and a number of basic values, some important subcultural differences in values or norms and in their interpretation may give rise to conflict. For example, freedom does not mean the same to most whites and to most Negroes in the United States. Whereas whites may stress *habeas corpus* and the Bill of Rights, Negroes tend to think first in terms of abolition of racial discrimination. Value pluralism, whether it is a result of cultural or of social pluralism, is an essential dimension in the study of social integration and conflict [7].

Finally, it is useful to consider pluralism in relation to *individuals* as distinct from values, institutions, and groups. Even though a society may be segmented into discrete corporate groups with distinct values and institutions, individuals may move back and forth in structural or cultural space. To use another racial illustration, the American Negro who passes for white on the job and returns to the ghetto in the evening is, in effect, commuting across a caste line. The same happens in the context of cultural pluralism. "Passing" does not negate the existence of racial or cultural cleavages; it simply means that some individuals can evade or manipulate the system without appreciably altering it.

Relative absence of consensus is one of the characteristics of pluralistic societies. This means that value consensus is not the necessary basis of social integration as claimed by some functionalists, notably by Talcott Parsons [8]. The case studies examined here suggest two important alternative bases of social integration which in combination have resulted in relatively stable societies. Pluralistic societies have often been held together by a mixture of *political coercion* and *economic interdependence.* The distribution of power in pluralistic societies frequently follows the major lines of cleavage between ethnic, caste, or racial groups. In some countries (like Switzerland) composed of culturally distinct but related groups, none of which has any clear linguistic, technological, social, or economic advantage over the others, a large measure of democracy can prevail. But most highly pluralistic societies have been characterized by a large degree of power concentration in one of the constituent groups and by the extensive use of coercive force against the other groups. Pluralism and tyranny, though complexly related, have tended to go together. A common instance of tyranny in pluralistic societies has been the political supremacy of a technologically superior group (often a minority) which used that superiority to monopolize the means of violence.

Coercion by itself is notoriously unstable as the basis of social integration, if indeed it can ever be found in pure form. However, combined with economic interdependence, it can be quite effective. If the dominant group not only monopolizes the political apparatus, but also controls key economic resources so that it reduces the economic self-sufficiency of subordinate groups (even at the barest subsistence level), then tyranny is difficult to overthrow. The case of South Africa offers a clear illustration. Coercion through mastery of the modern technology of violence, though widespread, is not sufficient to account for continued minority white rule. The other main factor that holds South Africa together in its present form is the utter dependence of the nonwhites on the economic resources controlled by the whites. Whites own and/or control virtually all capital, 87 per cent of the land, and all of the African labor through a complex machinery of "pass laws," "influx control," "job reservation," and "labor bureau." Keeping the African population, whether urban or rural, at a level close to starvation effectively limits strikes and other nonviolent techniques of opposition. Although it is true that the *prosperity* of the whites depends entirely on the nonwhites, the sheer day-to-day *survival* of the nonwhites depends directly on the industrial complex now controlled by the whites [9].

Slavery or latifundiary regimes are another illustration of

social integration   based on the combination of coercion and economic interdependence. Latifundiary monoculture profoundly undermined what had hitherto been subsistence economies and reduced the indigenous or slave population to "unviability" outside serfdom. Land expropriation and capitation taxes had similar effects on colonial territories of tropical Africa.

I shall attempt schematically to delineate somewhat further the major dimensions of pluralism at the four levels of analysis I have suggested. I do so with some reluctance because schemas have a deceptive air of finality and rigor that the embryonic stage of the present formulation hardly merits, and because schemas have a nasty way of pointing out all kinds of problems to which I cannot yet give satisfactory answers. One of the first and most basic questions concerns the independent variability of the dimensions. Some of the dimensions shown in Table 7.1 are clearly independently variable in that some societies are high on one and low on another, whereas others are either high or low on both. On the other hand, some of the "dimensions" are really facets of the same phenomenon viewed at different levels of analysis. The degree of independence of the variables remains to be established empirically.

Another problem that must remain open at this stage is the relative weight of these dimensions. I am not sure whether it would be useful to assign arithmetic values to them because the manipulative gain in making the variables commensurate may well be purchased at a staggering cost in one's ability to deal meaningfully with the subject under consideration. At the present stage, the schema simply allows us to say that society x is higher or lower than society y on variables l, m, and n. The schema also points to internal discrepancies between variables within a given society.

The trichotomous mode of presentation inevitably suggests a hidden assumption of linearity for each of the variables. The reality is almost certainly not so simple. Undoubtedly, significant thresholds and discontinuities remain to be determined empirically.

We must also point out that each of the four levels of analysis (groups, institutions, values, and individuals) has both a cultural and a social facet, although the value level is more "culturally loaded" than the others. (See Table 7.1 on pp. 142–143.)

Having pondered over the schema, the reader may legitimately ask: "So what?" The attempt to determine how pluralistic a society is is clearly not an end in itself. Implicit in the schema is the suggestion that pluralism be regarded as a set of independent variables helping us to understand such fundamental sociological questions as the genesis of group conflict, the bases of, and conditions for, social integration, the distribution and exercise of power, the establishment and maintenance of social stratification, and the dynamics of culture change and assimilation. In short, the analysis of pluralism is a somewhat new vantage point from which to approach the comparative study of whole societies and more specifically a conceptual framework for the understanding of complex, heterogeneous societies. Let us try to suggest briefly some of the dependent variables of pluralism.

Highly pluralistic societies frequently exhibit a set of interrelated characteristics. At the level of corporate groups there is political polarization; asymmetry in the distribution of power; heavy reliance on coercion by one of the groups; salience of conflict; economic interdependence based on inequality in the control of resources and rewards; and rigid stratification based on status ascription and role asymmetry.

At the level of institutions there are cleavages between relatively autonomous structures and relative lack of integration outside the economic and political sphere. Although there is great asymmetry of status, power, and wealth between groups, at the institutional level there is duplication and analogy of function as opposed to functional complementarity and differentiation. Integration between institutional structures is often made more difficult because the institutions are based on incompatible principles, even though they fulfill analogous functions in the respective groups to which they apply. For example, a kinship system that is based on primogeniture, prohibition of cousin marriage, bilateral descent, neolocality, and monogamy is difficult to integrate with one that stresses or enjoins inheritance from mother's brother to sister's son, matrilineal descent, avunculocal residence, polygyny, levirate, moiety exogamy, and prefer-

TABLE 7.1
Some Dimensions of Pluralism

Level of Analysis	Dimension	Degree of Pluralism		
		High	Medium	Low
Group Level	Number of ethnic, racial or caste groups	Many	Few	One
	Relative size of groups	No group a numerical majority	Large minorities (over 10 per cent)	Minorities absent or insignificantly small (less than 10 per cent)
	Geographical distribution of groups	Great regional and/or local concentration	Some concentration	Proportional spacial dispersion
	Clarity of group boundaries	Membership unambiguous and mutually exclusive	Presence of marginal cases	Membership ambiguous or overlapping
	Rigidity of group boundaries	Great rigidity. Ascribed membership. Rigid endogamy	Some rigidity but also some "passing"; some intermarriage	Flexibility; membership by achievement; no endogamy rules
Institutional Level	Range of institutional autonomy	Autonomous cultures with complete institutional structures	Institutional autonomy limited to specialized spheres (e.g, religion or family)	Single institutional structure. Culture coterminous with society

TABLE 7.1 (Continued)

Level of Analysis	Dimension	Degree of Pluralism		
		High	Medium	Low
	Degree of institutional multiplication	Multiple sets of homologous institutions	Limited number of homologous institutions (e.g., dualistic structure)	Single set of institutions
	Cultural distance between institutions	Historically unrelated traditions (e.g., Spanish and Maya)	Distinct but related tradition (e.g., Protestants and Catholics)	One tradition with only subcultural variants
	Institutional compatibility	Incompatible institutions (e.g., monogamy and polygyny)	Distinct but at least partially compatible institutions (e.g., Buddhism and Confucianism)	Single set of institutions
Value Level	Degree of consensus	Low	Medium	High
	Range of consensus	Narrow	Medium	Wide
	Compatibility of value systems	Distinct and incompatible values	Distinct but partially compatible values	Unitary value system or completely compatible values
Individual Level	Ease, speed and frequency of "passing"	Impossible	Possible but slow, difficult and/or infrequent	Easy, rapid and/or frequent
	Compatibility of group memberships	Incompatible	Marginal or role conflict situations	Compatible

ential cross-cousin marriage. Indeed, integration is virtually impossible at that level, short of cultural assimilation of one group by the other or at least considerable syncretism, that is, short of a reduction of pluralism.

At the level of values pluralistic societies are characterized by lack of consensus and frequently by direct conflict. In the case of cultural pluralism each ethnic group will have its system of values; the degree of fortuitous congruence between cultural value systems can vary widely, but anything approaching complete compatibility in all essentials is, of course, unlikely, unless the ethnic groups are closely related. In the case of social pluralism between racial, class, or caste groups which are not culturally distinct (or only minimally so), value dissension is likely to arise from inequalities in power, wealth, and status. A dialectic of group conflict frequently sets in, which, in turn, leads to a polarization of ideology and values or at least to a widely discrepant interpretation of common values.

Finally, at the level of individuals pluralistic societies are characterized by two differentiated networks of ties. Between members of different corporate groups, asymmetrical, functionally specific, segmentary, utilitarian relationships prevail, with great salience of the economic and political or administrative aspects of interaction. Within groups, relationships tend to be more symmetrical, functionally diffuse, affective, and not as predominantly instrumental or utilitarian. Certain types of relations that stress these qualities most strongly, such as commensality and marriage, are *de facto* restricted to one's own group or even severely tabooed between members of different groups.

Before concluding this chapter let us turn briefly to two more problems. The first concerns the relationship between the theory of pluralism and the paternalistic-competitive typology of race relations. Clearly, both types of race relations refer to pluralistic societies insofar as race is a special instance of social pluralism. There are, however, important differences in the modalities of pluralism (and more particularly in the interplay between social and cultural pluralism) between the two types of race relations.

Under a paternalistic regime close symbiosis between the dominant group and at least a segment of the subordinate group or groups makes for a reduction of cultural pluralism through acculturation and sometimes also of racial pluralism through miscegenation. Miscegenation by itself does not always have that effect as shown by the United States and South Africa. It is simply a facilitating condition. The underlying bases of pluralism in a paternalistic system are the wide discrepancies in status, power, and wealth between the racial groups, rather than institutional parallelism or segmentation which is more prevalent in a competitive system. Furthermore, racial pluralism in a paternalistic system is maintained partially by force and economic interdependence, but also by a measure of consensus resulting from acculturation and internalization of inferior status by the subordinate groups.

In a competitive situation, on the other hand, conflict and coercion are more prevalent, and concerted attempts are often made by the dominant group to perpetuate or even extend social pluralism (even in the absence of cultural pluralism) and to counteract any economic or other trends toward greater social integration. Segregation and discrimination are the foremost mechanisms for the preservation of racial pluralism in the presence of cultural assimilation and other integrative pressures. Thus a competitive situation is one in which the ruling group deliberately maintains social pluralism by force in order to protect its privileged position. Paternalistic societies, on the other hand, are racially and frequently culturally pluralistic, more as a consequence of original disparities in their constituent groups than because of dominant group policy. Coercive maintenance and extension of pluralism along racial lines enter when the subordinate group threatens the status of the upper caste, that is, typically in a competitive situation.

The last problem to which I shall briefly turn concerns the relationship between the concept of pluralism as I have presented it here and the more common use of the term in the North American political and social science literature [10]. The reader familiar with this latter tradition will of necessity have been disconcerted by my treatment of the subject, because I seem to ascribe to pluralism properties opposite to those mentioned by most American scholars.

Briefly stated, the traditional view of pluralism identifies the concept with democracy. In pluralistic societies a multiplicity of

autonomous organizations and interest groups representing different spheres of activity (religion, labor, politics, business, and
so on) compete freely with each other for political control. This
situation is contrasted with the totalitarian society in which the
state, through the ruling single party, attempts to subdue or
incorporate all other organizations and groups and to reduce the
sphere of individual or group autonomy. Pluralism is held to be
conducive to democracy because the many organizations and
groups have overlapping and not mutually exclusive member-
ships; because the political alignment of various groups shifts
with issues; and because such power as is wielded by specific
groups is cancelled out by the countervailing power of other
groups. The democratic polity, according to this conception, is
simultaneously an arbiter of the competitive game between organized groups, an open arena for such a competition, the stake of
the game, and the product of the prior outcomes of the game.
The structure of the polity itself is plural, with separation of
powers, checks, and balances, and other safeguards against
monopolization of power.

Two assumptions underlie this concept of democratic pluralism, those of equilibrium and consensus about ultimate values.
The polity is held together by an intricate balance of cross-cutting
and multiple affiliations and by adherence to a common system of
values and of rules of the game that define the legitimate
boundaries of opposition and transcend divergences of interests.

Is this the same phenomenon as what I have called pluralism?
The answer, I think, is that there is some overlap of meaning, but
only a partial one. Insofar as the traditional model of pluralism
(as contrasted with the one used here) deals with distinct and
competing corporate groups, there is some overlap of meaning.
Insofar as the traditional model regards as pluralistic what are
simply functionally differentiated sectors of an integrated structure (e.g., various occupational groupings) it departs from my
usage of pluralism here.

The traditional concept of pluralism wrongly identifies that
phenomenon with democracy for three basic reasons:

1. As just suggested, it fails to distinguish between pluralism
and functional differentiation.

2. It is based principally on nineteenth century United States, that is, on a society which, in our terms, shows only a moderate degree of social pluralism and a small degree of cultural pluralism. From this extremely limited perspective, scholars unduly generalize and postulate a general relationship between pluralism and democracy.

3. It fails to take into account the deepest social cleavage in the United States and hence the most significant way in which that country is socially pluralistic, namely the color bar. It does violence to the facts unqualifiedly to describe the American polity as democratic when, in respect to the main dimension of pluralism, it has been blatantly oppressive. Until recently the United States was a democracy of sorts, but only for the master race.

The safest conclusion is that there is no necessary or universal association of pluralism with either democracy or tyranny. There are a few cases of moderately pluralistic polities that have also been fairly democratic, such as Switzerland or Belgium. India probably represents an extreme case in that it is characterized by a high degree of both pluralism and democracy. But many highly homogeneous societies, for example, a number of stateless and classless African societies like the Nuer, have also been quite democratic. It is true that modern totalitarian societies such as Nazi or Fascist regimes have ruthlessly suppressed all forms of pluralism to the extent of genocide and have enforced a policy of *Gleichschaltung* ("uniformization"). It is equally true, however, that most of the world's highly pluralistic societies have been quite undemocratic, albeit in a very different way from modern totalitarianism. For example, the South African government, far from trying to create a monolithic, homogeneous, tightly integrated state and to mobilize the entire population for united action, makes use of tyranny to achieve precisely opposite ends, namely to maximize cultural, social, territorial, and institutional fragmentation and cleavage. Both forms of tyranny attempt to divide and rule, but what totalitarianism seeks to obtain by atomizing and homogenizing the citizenry, pluralistic forms of despotism endeavor to achieve through division into antagonistic groups.

In this chapter I have tried to show how the study of race and ethnic relations can be integrated in a broader theoretical framework. I have argued that the concept of pluralism, as defined in Chapter 1, is of great value in analyzing multiracial societies and in relating race to other dimensions of social cleavage and conflict. In the more specific analysis of the racial dimensions of society, our typology of race relations has proven useful in comparing multiracial societies with one another, in understanding the complex structures of these societies, and in tracing the processes of change that transformed these societies over time. Space limitations have forced me to trim the description of the four case studies down to a bare outline and to reduce the analytical and theoretical parts to a mere sketch.

In conclusion, and irrespective of whether the specific ideas contained in this book prove useful, I should like to suggest that the study of race relations must meet certain conditions in order to progress beyond its rather pedestrian, applied, and atheoretical present state.

1. Individual scholars must develop sufficient modesty, integrity, and self-insight to abandon chimerical claims to objectivity and to stop mascarading as experts in "human engineering" when, in fact, they act almost invariably as ideologues as soon as they try to apply their knowledge to practical situations. Direct political involvement and ideological commitment are perfectly justified but not under the cover of "science." (Economics is probably the only social science that can make an honestly uninflated claim to expertise, but, even there, only within narrow limits.)

2. Race must be clearly recognized as a *subjective* and *social* reality and as a special instance of several different classes of phenomena depending on the approach used. That is, race must not be unduly reified as something external or prior to the particular social system under study. Race, as defined here, has no objective reality independent of its social definition. Vice-versa, "race," in the sense of subspecies of *homo sapiens* has no social significance.

3. Race relations must also be studied holistically and macro-sociologically, that is, in the context of total societies. This is

obviously not the only legitimate approach to the problem, but unless more specific studies are complemented by a broader type of investigation, the accumulation of knowledge is bound to remain piecemeal. Certain problems simply cannot be solved by questionnaires, attitude scales, or small group experiments. Total societies are meaningful and, for many purposes, irreducible units.

4. Race relations must be studied cross-culturally. Human diversity is such that the limits of the existing spectrum on any given variable and the nature of interrelationships between parts or dimensions of social systems can be specified only by making the sample as close in size to the universe as possible, or failing that, by judiciously selecting extreme as well as modal cases. Social science theory is still tentative enough that almost any "special case" forces one to reformulate prior generalizations.

5. Race relations must be studied cross-temporally. That is, social scientists must study race historically, tracing developments in given societies through time while at the same time resisting the temptation of a facile retreat to pure historical description for its own sake.

If I may perpetrate in conclusion a semantic abomination, I should say that this program is merely a general plea for historico-comparative macrosociology. This is hardly an original plea, and a number of scholars are doing what I suggest. But I believe that there is an imbalance in the allocation of intellectual and economic resources, favoring studies which use quantitative or experimental methods and which are minute and fragmentary in scope. This imbalance continues to prevail in spite of the fact that intellectual returns have clearly not been proportional to the money and time invested in the expensive search for quantifiable trivia. The "principal investigator" of the mammoth research project recalls the conquistador in quest of the mythical Eldorado. Like Cortés he returns with just enough gold to convince his peers and the foundations that there is a lot more to be found, and like Cortés, in the process of feeding social reality through gargantuan fact-digesting computers, he often melts down priceless jewels into crude ingots.

NOTES

[1] Gordon W. Allport, *The Nature of Prejudice.*
[2] The reader should refer back to the last section of Chapter I for a definition of cultural and social pluralism.
[3] Cf. Oscar Handlin. *Race and Nationality in American Life,* Chapter One.
[4] For analytical purposes, we may, in addition to the two extreme cases of cultural pluralism just mentioned, conceive of an intermediate one, that of coexistence of distinct but historically *related* ethnic groups. A number of European countries would fall in that category, for example, Belgium, Switzerland, and Yugoslavia. Another useful distinction is that between *stable* cultural pluralism where two or more groups live side by side without any apparent tendency for any of them to disappear in the foreseeable future. *Unstable* cultural pluralism, on the other hand, would describe conditions in countries like Australia, Argentina, or the United States where immigrant groups may retain some cultural distinctiveness for one or two generations, but eventually merge into the dominant culture. I have dealt more extensively and systematically with the concepts of social and cultural pluralism in three other papers: "Pluralisme Social et Culturel," "Pluralism and the Polity, A Theoretical Exploration," and "Toward a Sociology of Africa." See also, M. G. Smith's article "Social and Cultural Pluralism."
[5] Cf. Melville J. Herskovits, *The American Negro.*
[6] Cf. E. Franklin Frazier, *The Negro Family in the United States.*
[7] See a more extensive treatment of the role of value consensus in problems of social integration and conflict in my article "Dialectic and Functionalism."
[8] Cf. Talcott Parsons, *The Social System.*
[9] There is another side to the effect of urbanization and industrialization on apartheid. Although these trends have woven closer ties of "reluctant interdependence" between racial groups, these trends have also unleashed sources of conflict and tensions which undermine the rigid system of racial castes.
[10] This other tradition has a distinguished intellectual history that goes back to Alexis de Tocqueville. Among many more recent social and political scientists who have ascribed to pluralism properties antithetical to the ones mentioned here are Raymond Aron, W. Kornhauser, William McCord, and Edward Shils. Cf. in particular Kornhauser's *The Politics of Mass Society;* Shils' *The Torment of Secrecy;* and McCord's *The Springtime of Freedom.*

Selected Bibliography

General and Theoretical*

Adorno, T. W., Else Frenkel-Brunswik, Daniel J. Levinson, 2nd, and R. Nevitt Sanford, *The Authoritarian Personality*, New York: Harper, 1950.

Allport, Gordon W., *The Nature of Prejudice*, Cambridge, Mass.: Addison-Wesley, 1954.

Aubery, Pierre, *Milieux Juifs de la France Contemporaine*. Paris: Plon, 1962.

Berry, Brewton, *Race and Ethnic Relations*. Boston: Houghton Mifflin, 1958.

Bettelheim, Bruno, and Morris Janowitz, *Dynamics of Prejudice*, New York: Harper, 1950.

Christie, Richard, and Marie Jahoda, eds., *Studies in the Scope and Method of "The Authoritarian Personality."* New York: Free Press, 1954.

Comas, Juán, *Racial Myths*. Paris: UNESCO, 1952.

Coser, Lewis A., *The Functions of Social Conflict*. New York: The Free Press, 1956.

Cox, Oliver C., *Caste, Class and Race*. Garden City, New York: Doubleday, 1948.

Dahrendorf, Ralf, *Class and Class Conflict in Industrial Society*. Stanford: Stanford University Press, 1959.

Dahrendorf, Ralf, "Toward a Theory of Social Conflict," *Journal of Conflict Resolution*, 2, 170–183, 1958.

Dollard, John, et al., *Frustration and Aggression*. New Haven, Conn.: Yale University Press, 1939.

* This section includes works of different kinds. Besides general theoretical and comparative works, it also includes books and articles based principally on research in one or more of the four countries for which there is a separate section of the bibliography, if the principal contribution of these studies is in the theoretical field. This section also lists specific studies of countries other than the United States, Mexico, Brazil, and South Africa.

Durkheim, Emile, *The Division of Labor in Society*. New York: Macmillan, 1933.

Frazier, E. Franklin, *Race and Culture Contacts in the Modern World*. New York: Knopf, 1957.

Gann, Stanley M., and Carleton S. Coon, "On the Number of Races of Mankind," *American Anthropologist*, 57, 996–1001, 1955.

Gluckman, Max, *Custom and Conflict in Africa*. Oxford: Blackwell, 1955.

Hofstadter, Richard, *Social Darwinism in American Thought*. New York: Braziller, 1959.

Horton, John, "Order and Conflict Theories of Social Problems as Competing Ideologies," *American Journal of Sociology*, 71, 701–713, 1966.

Johnson, John T., ed., *Continuity and Change in Latin America*. Stanford: Stanford University Press, 1964.

Kornhauser, W., *The Politics of Mass Society*. London: Routledge and Kegan Paul, 1960.

Lieberson, Stanley, "A Societal Theory of Race and Ethnic Relations," *American Sociological Review*, 26, 902–910, 1961.

Lind, Andrew W., ed., *Race Relations in World Perspective*. Honolulu: University of Hawaii Press, 1955.

Mason, Philip, *An Essay on Racial Tension*. London and New York: Royal Institute of International Affairs, 1954.

McCord, William, *The Springtime of Freedom, The Evolution of Developing Societies*. New York: Oxford University Press, 1965.

Merton, Robert K., "Discrimination and the American Creed," in R. M. MacIver, ed., *Discrimination and National Welfare*. New York: Harper, 1949.

Mitchell, J. Clyde, *Tribalism and the Plural Society*. London: Oxford University Press, 1960.

Montagu, M. F. Ashley, *Statement on Race*. New York: Schuman, 1951.

Montagu, M. F. Ashley, *Introduction to Physical Anthropology*. Springfield, Ill., Thomas, 1960.

Padilla, Elena, "Peasants, Plantations and Pluralism," *Annals of the New York Academy of Sciences*, 83, 837–842, 1959–1960.

Park, Robert Ezra, *Race and Culture*. New York: The Free Press, 1950.

Parsons, Talcott, *The Social System*. New York: The Free Press, 1951.

Shibutani, Tamotsu, and Kian M. Kwan, *Ethnic Stratification, A Comparative Approach*. New York: Macmillan, 1965.

Shils, Edward, *The Torment of Secrecy*. London: Heinemann, 1956.

Simpson, George E., and J. Milton Yinger, *Racial and Cultural Minorities: An Analysis of Prejudice and Discrimination*. New York: Harper, 1953.

Smith, M. G., *The Plural Society in the British West Indies*. Berkeley: University of California Press, 1965.

Smith, M. G., "Social and Cultural Pluralism," *Annals of the New York Academy of Sciences*, 83, 763–777, 1959–1960.

Smith, M. G., *Stratification in Grenada*. Berkeley: University of California Press, 1965.

Snyder, Louis L., *The Idea of Racialism*. Princeton, N. J.: D. Van Nostrand, 1962.

Tannenbaum, Frank, *Slave and Citizen, The Negro in the Americas*. New York: Knopf, 1947.

van den Berghe, Pierre L., ed., *Africa: Social Problems of Change and Conflict*. San Francisco: Chandler, 1965.

van den Berghe, Pierre L., "Dialectic and Functionalism, Toward a Theoretical Synthesis," *American Sociological Review*, 28, 695–705, 1963.

van den Berghe, Pierre L., "The Dynamics of Racial Prejudice; An Ideal-Type Dichotomy," *Social Forces*, 37, 138–141, 1958.

van den Berghe, Pierre L., "Paternalistic versus Competitive Race Relations: An Ideal-Type Approach," in Bernard Segal, ed., *Racial and Ethnic Relations: Selected Readings*. New York: Crowell, 1966, pp. 53–69.

van den Berghe, Pierre L., "Pluralism and the Polity, A Theoretical Exploration," in Leo Kuper and M. G. Smith, eds., *Pluralism in Africa*. Berkeley, University of California Press (in press).

van den Berghe, Pierre L., "Pluralisme Social et Culturel," *Cahiers Internationaux de Sociologie* (in press).

van den Berghe, Pierre L., "Racialism and Assimilation in Africa and the Americas," *Southwestern Journal of Anthropology*, 19, 424–432, 1963.

van den Berghe, Pierre L., "Toward a Sociology of Africa," *Social Forces*, 43, 11–18, 1964.

Wagley, Charles, and Marvin Harris, *Minorities in the New World*. New York: Columbia University Press, 1958.

Wallerstein, Immanuel, *Africa, The Politics of Independence*. New York: Vintage, 1961.

Wallerstein, Immanuel, ed. *Social Change, The Colonial Situation*. New York: Wiley, 1966.

Williams, Robin M., *The Reduction of Intergroup Tension*. New York: Social Science Research Council, 1947.

Wirth, Louis, "The Problem of Minority Groups," in Ralph Linton, ed., *The Science of Man in the World Crisis*. New York: Columbia University Press, 1945.

Worsley, Peter, *The Third World*. London: Weidenfeld and Nicholson, 1964.

Mexico

Adams, Richard N., et al., *Social Change in Latin America Today*. New York: Random House, 1960.

Aguirre Beltrán, Gonzalo, *La Población Negra de México, 1519–1810*. México D. F.: Ediciones Fuente Cultural, 1946.

Aguirre Beltrán, Gonzalo, *El Proceso de Aculturación*. México: Universidad Nacional Autónoma de México, 1957.

Basauri, Carlos, *La Población Indígena de México*. México: Secretaria de Educación Pública, 1940.

Beals, Ralph, "Social Stratification in Latin America," *American Journal of Sociology*, 58, 1953.

Caso, Alfonso, et al., *Métodos y Resultados de la Política Indigenista en México*. México: Memórias del Instituto Nacional Indígenista, **6**, 1954.

Cline, Howard F., *Mexico, Revolution to Evolution, 1940–1960*. New York: Oxford University Press, 1963.

Colby, Benjamin N., *Ethnic Relations in the Chiapas Highlands*. Museum of New Mexico Press, 1966.

Colby, Benjamin N., and Pierre L. van den Berghe, "Ethnic Relations in Southeastern Mexico," *American Anthropologist*, **63**, 772–792, 1961.

de la Fuente, Julio, "Definición, Pase y Desaparición del Indio en México," *América Indígena*, **7**, No. 1, 1947.

de la Fuente, Julio, *Relaciones Interétnicas*. México: Instituto Nacional Indígenista, 1955.

Diaz del Castillo, Bernal, *The True History of the Conquest of New Spain*. London: Hakluyt Society, 1908–1916.

González Casanova, Pablo, *La Democracía en México*. México: Ediciones Era, 1965.

González Casanova, Pablo, "Sociedad Plural, Colonialismo Interno y Desarrollo, *América Latina*, **6**, No. 3, 15–32, 1963.

Hayner, Norman S., *New Patterns in Old Mexico*. New Haven, Conn.: College and University Press, 1966.

Lewis, Oscar, *Five Families*. New York: Wiley, 1962.

Lewis, Oscar, *Life in a Mexican Village, Tepoztlán Restudied*. Urbana: University of Illinois Press, 1951.

Lewis, Oscar, *Tepoztlán, Village in Mexico*. New York: Holt, Rinehart and Winston, 1960.

Paz, Octavio, *The Labyrinth of Solitude, Life and Thought in Mexico*. New York: Grove, 1961.

Ramos, Samuel, *Profile of Man and Culture in Mexico*. New York: McGraw-Hill, 1963.

Redfield, Robert, *The Primitive World and Its Transformations*. Ithaca: Cornell University Press, 1957.

Redfield, Robert, *Tepoztlán, A Mexican Village*. Chicago: University of Chicago Press, 1941.

Tax, Sol, ed., *The Heritage of Conquest*. New York: Free Press, 1952.

Tumin, Melvin, *Caste in a Peasant Society*. Princeton, N. J.: Princeton University Press, 1952.

van den Berghe, Pierre L., and Benjamin Colby, "Ladino-Indian Relations in the Highlands of Chiapas, Mexico," *Social Forces*, **40**, 63–71, 1961.

Vogt, Evon Z., ed., *Los Zinacantecos*. México: Instituto Nacional Indígenista, 1966.

Whiteford, Andrew H., *Two Cities of Latin America*. Garden City, N. Y.: Doubleday, 1964.

Brazil

Bastide, Roger, "Race Relations in Brazil, São Paulo," *Courier*, UNESCO, **5**, Nos. 8–9, 1952.

SELECTED BIBLIOGRAPHY 155

Bastide, Roger, and Florestan Fernandes, *Brancos e Negros em São Paulo*. São Paulo: Companhia Editora Nacional, 1959.

Bastide, Roger, and Pierre van den Berghe, "Stereotypes, Norms and Interracial Behavior in São Paulo, Brazil," *American Sociological Review*, **22**, 689–694, 1957.

DaCosta Pinto, L. A., "Race Relations in Brazil, Rio de Janeiro," *Courier*, UNESCO, **5**, Nos. 8–9, 1952.

de Azevedo, Fernando, *Brazilian Culture*. New York: Macmillan, 1950.

de Azevedo, Thales, *Les Elites de Couleur dans une Ville Brésilienne*. Paris: UNESCO, 1953.

de Moraes, Evaristo, *A Escravidão Africana no Brasil*. São Paulo: Companhia Editora Nacional, 1933.

Freyre, Gilberto, *The Mansions and the Shanties*. New York: Knopf, 1963.

Freyre, Gilberto, *The Masters and the Slaves*. New York: Knopf, 1964.

Freyre, Gilberto, *New World in the Tropics*. New York: Knopf, 1959.

Horowitz, Irving L., *Revolution in Brazil*. New York: Dutton, 1964.

Hutchinson, William H., *Village and Plantation Life in Northeastern Brazil*. Seattle: University of Washington Press, 1957.

Lowrie, S. A., "Racial and National Intermarriage in a Brazilian City," *American Journal of Sociology*, **44**, 684–698, 1939.

Marchant, Alexander, *From Barter to Slavery*. Baltimore: Johns Hopkins, 1942.

Nash, Roy, *The Conquest of Brazil*. New York: Harcourt Brace, 1926.

Oberg, Kalervo, "The Marginal Peasant in Rural Brazil," *American Anthropologist*, **67**, No. 6, 1417–1427, December 1965.

Pandiá Calogeras, João, *A History of Brazil*. Chapel Hill: University of North Carolina Press, 1939.

Pierson, Donald, *Negroes in Brazil, A Study of Race Contact at Bahia*. Chicago: University of Chicago Press, 1942.

Smith, Thomas Lynn, *Brazil, People and Institutions*. Baton Rouge: Louisiana State University Press, 1963.

Smith, Thomas Lynn, and Alexander Marchant, eds., *Brazil, Portrait of Half a Continent*. New York: Dryden, 1951.

Wagley, Charles, *Amazon Town, A Study of Man in the Tropics*. New York: Macmillan, 1964.

Wagley, Charles, *Brazil, Crisis and Change*. New York: Foreign Policy Association, 1964.

Wagley, Charles, ed., *Race and Class in Rural Brazil*. Paris: UNESCO, 1952.

Willems, Emilio, "Racial Attitudes in Brazil," *American Journal of Sociology*, **54**, 402–408, 1949.

United States*

Barron, Milton L., *American Minorities*. New York: Knopf, 1957.

Cash, W. J., *The Mind of the South*. Garden City, N. Y.: Doubleday, 1954.

* For a more extensive bibliography of social science research on race relations in the United States, see Thomas F. Pettigrew, *A Profile of the Negro American*.

Davis, Allison W., B. B. Gardner and M. R. Gardner, *Deep South*. Chicago: University of Chicago Press, 1941.

Deutsch, M., and M. Collins, *Interracial Housing*. Minneapolis: University of Minnesota Press, 1951.

Dollard, John, *Caste and Class in a Southern Town*. New Haven, Conn.: Yale University Press, 1937.

Doyle, Bertram W., *The Etiquette of Race Relations in the South*. Chicago: University of Chicago Press, 1937.

Drake, St. Clair, and Horace R. Cayton, *Black Metropolis*. New York: Harcourt, Brace and Company, 1945.

DuBois, W. E. B., *Black Reconstruction*. New York: Russell and Russell, 1935.

Elkins, Stanley M., *Slavery, A Problem in American Institutional and Intellectual Life*. New York: Grossett and Dunlap, 1963.

Essien-Udom, E. U., *Black Nationalism*. New York: Dell, 1962.

Franklin, John Hope, *From Slavery to Freedom, A History of American Negroes*. New York: Knopf, 1952.

Frazier, E. Franklin, *Black Bourgeoisie*. New York: Free Press, 1957.

Frazier, E. Franklin, *The Negro Family in the United States*. New York: Citadel, 1948.

Frazier, E. Franklin, *The Negro in the United States*. New York: Macmillan, 1957.

Ginzberg, Eli, and Alfred S. Eichner, *The Troublesome Presence, American Democracy and the Negro*. New York: Free Press, 1964.

Glazer, Nathan, and Daniel P. Moynihan, *Beyond the Melting Pot*. Cambridge, Mass.: M.I.T. and Harvard University Press, 1963.

Gordon, Milton M., *Assimilation in American Life, The Role of Race, Religion and National Origins*. New York: Oxford University Press, 1964.

Gossett, Thomas F., *Race, The History of an Idea in America*. Dallas: Southern Methodist University Press, 1963.

Handlin, Oscar, *Race and Nationality in American Life*. Garden City, N. Y.: Doubleday, 1957.

Herskovits, Melville J., *The American Negro*. New York: Knopf, 1928.

Herskovits, Melville J., *The Myth of the Negro Past*. Boston: Beacon Press, 1958.

Johnson, Charles S., *Patterns of Negro Segregation*. New York: London, Harper and Brothers, 1943.

Johnson, Charles S., *Shadow of the Plantation*. Chicago: The University of Chicago Press, 1934.

Kardiner, A., and L. Ovesey, *The Mark of Oppression*. New York: Norton, 1951.

Klineberg, Otto, *Characteristics of the American Negro*. New York: London, Harper, 1944.

Litwack, Leon F., *North of Slavery, The Negro in the Free States, 1790–1860*. Chicago: University of Chicago Press, 1961.

Mack, Raymond M., ed., *Race, Class and Power*. New York: American Book, 1963.

Myers, Gustavus, *History of Bigotry in the United States.* New York: Putnam, 1960.

Myrdal, Gunnar, *An American Dilemma.* New York: Harper, 1944.

Olmsted, Frederick L., *The Slave States.* New York: Capricorn, 1959.

Pettigrew, Thomas F., *A Profile of the Negro American.* Princeton, N. J.: D. Van Nostrand, 1964.

Pettigrew, Thomas F., *Regional Differences in Anti-Negro Prejudice,* Harvard University, Ph. D. Thesis, 1956.

Phillips, Ulrich B., *Life and Labor in the Old South.* Boston: Little, Brown, 1963.

Rose, Arnold, *The Negro in America.* Boston: Beacon Press, 1959.

Rose, Arnold, ed., *Race Prejudice and Discrimination.* New York: Knopf, 1951.

Rose, Peter I., *They and We.* New York: Random House, 1964.

Schermerhorn, R. A., *These Our People.* Boston: Heath, 1949.

Segal, Bernard E., ed., *Racial and Ethnic Relations.* New York: Crowell, 1966.

Silberman, Charles E., *Crisis in Black and White.* New York: Random House, 1964.

Simpson, George E., and J. Milton Yinger, *Racial and Cultural Minorities.* New York: Harper, 1965.

Smith, Lillian, *Killers of the Dream.* Garden City, N. Y.: Doubleday, 1963.

Stampp, Kenneth M., *The Peculiar Institution, Slavery in the Ante-Bellum South.* New York: Vintage, 1964.

Vander Zanden, James W., *American Minority Relations.* New York: Ronald Press, 1963.

Williams, Robin M., *Strangers Next Door, Ethnic Relations in American Communities.* Englewood Cliffs, N. J.: Prentice Hall, 1964.

Wirth, Louis, *The Ghetto.* Chicago: University of Chicago Press, 1928.

Woodward, C. Vann, *The Strange Career of Jim Crow.* New York: Oxford University Press, 1955.

Yinger, J. Milton, *A Minority Group in American Society.* New York: McGraw-Hill, 1965.

*South Africa**

Botha, C. G., *Social Life in the Cape Colony in the 18th Century.* Cape Town and Johannesburg: Juta, 1926.

Carter, Gwendolen M., *The Politics of Inequality, South Africa since 1948.* New York: Praeger, 1958.

De Kiewiet, C. W., *A History of South Africa, Social and Economic.* Oxford: Clarendon, 1941.

De Kiewiet, C. W., *The Anatomy of South African Misery.* London, New York, Toronto: Oxford University Press, 1956.

* A more extensive bibliography of social science research on South African race relations can be found in my book *South Africa, A Study in Conflict.*

Dvorin, Eugene P., *Racial Separation in South Africa.* Chicago: University of Chicago Press, 1952.

Edwards, Isobel E., *Towards Emancipation: A Study in South African Slavery.* Cardiff, Wales: Gomerian, 1942.

Hellmann, Ellen, ed., *Handbook of Race Relations in South Africa.* Cape Town, London, New York: Oxford University Press, 1949.

Holleman, J. F., J. W. Mann, and Pierre L. van den Berghe, "A Rhodesian White Minority under Threat," *The Journal of Social Psychology,* **57**, 315–338, 1962.

Horrell, Muriel, *A Survey of Race Relations in South Africa.* Johannesburg, S. A. Institute of Race Relations (annual).

Hunter, Monica, *Reaction to Conquest.* London: Oxford University Press, 1936.

Kuper, Hilda, *Indian People in Natal.* Durban: University of Natal Press, 1960.

Kuper, Hilda, *The Uniform of Colour.* Johannesburg: Witwatersrand University Press, 1947.

Kuper, Leo, *An African Bourgeoisie.* New Haven, Conn.: Yale University Press, 1965.

Kuper, Leo, *Passive Resistance in South Africa.* London: Jonathan Cape, 1956.

Kuper, Leo, Hilstan Watts, and Ronald Davies, *Durban, A Study in Racial Ecology.* London: Jonathan Cape, 1958.

Luthuli, Albert, *Let My People Go.* New York: McGraw-Hill, 1962.

MacCrone, I. D., *Race Attitudes in South Africa.* London, New York, Toronto: Oxford University Press, 1937.

Marais, J. S., *The Cape Coloured People, 1652–1937.* London, New York, Toronto: Longmans, Green, 1939.

Marquard, Leo, *The Peoples and Policies of South Africa.* London, New York, Cape Town: Oxford University Press, 1952.

Mayer, Philip, "Migrancy and the Study of Africans in Towns," *American Anthropologist,* **64**, 576–592, 1962.

Mayer, Philip, *Townsmen or Tribesmen.* Cape Town: Oxford University Press, 1961.

Ngubane, Jordan K., *An African Explains Apartheid.* New York: Praeger, 1963.

Paton, Alan, *Cry, the Beloved Country.* New York: Scribner, 1948.

Patterson, Sheila, *Colour and Culture in South Africa.* London: Routledge and Kegan Paul, 1953.

Patterson, Sheila, *The Last Trek.* London: Routledge and Kegan Paul, 1957.

Rhoodie, N. J., and H. J. Venter, *Apartheid: A Socio-Historical Exposition of the Origin and Development of the Apartheid Idea.* Amsterdam: De Bussy, 1960.

Sundkler, Bengt G. M., *Bantu Prophets in South Africa.* London: Lutterworth Press, 1948.

van den Berghe, Pierre L., *Caneville, The Social Structure of a South African Town.* Middletown, Conn.: Wesleyan University Press, 1964.

van den Berghe, Pierre L., "Miscegenation in South Africa," *Cahiers d'Etudes Africaines,* 4, 68–84, 1960.

van den Berghe, Pierre L., "Race Attitudes in Durban, South Africa," *Journal of Social Psychology,* 57, 55–72, 1962.

van den Berghe, Pierre L., *South Africa, A Study in Conflict.* Middletown, Conn.: Wesleyan University Press, 1965.

Vatcher, William H., *White Laager.* New York: Praeger, 1965.

Wilson, Monica, and Archie Mafeje, *Langa, A Study of Social Groups in an African Township.* Cape Town: Oxford University Press, 1963.

Index

Portland, Oregon, 21
Portuguese, 51, 56, 60, 61, 63,
    64-65, 68, 76, 114, 115, 116,
    125
Positivism, 2, 8
Power, 102-103, 122, 139, 141
Prejudice, 6, 18-21, 24, 27-28, 30,
    32, 39, 52, 60, 69-75, 86, 87, 99,
    129, 130, 132
Prohibition of Mixed Marriages
    Act, 108, 111
Proletarian lynching, 91
Prostitution, 98
Protestantism, 105, 115, 124, 125
Psychoanalysis, 18, 19, 65
Public Safety Act, 109
Puebla, 58
Puerto Rico, 14, 79

Quetzalcoatl, 43
Quilombos, 63, 67

Race, definition of, 9-10, 22, 62,
    148
Race, theories of, 1-37
Race riots, 30, 32, 92, 128
Racism, definition of, 11, 23
Racism, distribution of, 11-18, 56
Racism, Golden Age of, 87
Racism, ideology of, 13, 15-18,
    54, 55, 56
Racism, origins of, 11-18
Racism, psychodynamics of, 18-21
Radical Republicans, 84, 85
Recife, 62
Reconstruction Era, 5, 84-85, 88,
    89
Redfield, Robert, 40, 58
Reforma, 53
Repartimiento, 43, 44
Reservation of Separate Amenities
    Act, 104
Revolts, slave, 28, 32, 67-68, 82-83
Revolution, American, 17, 53, 77
Revolution, French, 17, 77
Revolution, Mexican, 38, 43, 44,
    53-54, 119, 127
Revolution of rising expectations, 92,
    129

Rhodesia, Northern, 39
Rhoodie, N. J., 111
Rio de Janeiro, 61, 62, 63, 70, 74
Rio Grande, 43
Ritual kinship, 54
Roles, racial, 27, 32, 89, 122, 126
Rondon, Candido Mariano da Silva, 70
Roosevelt, Franklin D., 92
Roosevelt, Theodore, 13, 16, 87, 94
Rose, Peter I., 95
Rotary Club, 21
Rwanda, 12

Salvador de Bahia, 60, 62
San Luis Potosí, 58
São Paulo, 62, 63, 68, 70, 72, 73, 74
Scapegoating, 19, 30, 32
Secondary cultural pluralism, 135-
    136
Segregation, 22, 27, 30, 32, 50, 67,
    70, 73, 88-90, 92, 94, 97, 104,
    107, 108, 110, 113, 114, 120,
    128, 129, 130, 135, 145
Senegalese, 24
Senzala, 65
Sertão, 62, 68
Serviço de Proteção aos Indios, 70
Sevilla, 46
Share-cropping, 87, 125
Shibutani, Tamotsu, 4
Shils, Edward, 150
Silberman, Charles E., 95
Simpson, George, E., 25, 38, 39, 40
Slave trade, 60-61, 78, 83, 96-97,
    113, 117
Slavery, 15, 16, 17, 18, 26, 28, 46,
    51, 52, 59, 60, 61, 62, 64-68,
    69, 77-84, 97, 111, 113, 116-117,
    119, 123, 124, 125, 132, 133, 135,
    137, 139-140
Smith, Lillian, 95
Smith, M. G., 12-13, 38, 40, 150
Smuts, Jan, 130
Social change, 36, 37, 68, 84-86,
    91-94, 112, 126, 129, 141, 148
Social class (*see also* Stratification),
    10, 18, 29, 31, 53, 54, 55, 60,
    68, 69, 72, 73, 81, 89, 92, 105,
    106-107, 119, 127

Xhosa, 106, 114

Yinger, J. Milton, 25, 38, 39, 40, 95
Yucatán, 58
Yugoslavia, 150

Zambaigo, 49
Zapotecs, 53, 58
Zaria, 13
Zulu, 100, 106, 114

HT 1521 .V3 1967 45642 c1

Van den Berghe, Pierre L.

Race and racism

HT 1521 .V3 1967 45642 c1

Van den Berghe, Pierre L.

Race and racism